"Caroline Pignat has prepared a wonderful reflection on God's love for all people, inviting young people to take a closer look at the riches of our faith tradition. She includes words of wisdom from Sacred Scripture, saints, and gems from magisterial teaching. Caroline accompanies young people as they ponder their relationship with God, encouraging them to know how much God loves them and showing them how they were created to love, know, and serve God. This text is an excellent resource for anyone involved in youth ministry."

JOSEPHINE LOMBARDI, Ph.D., Associate Professor of Systematic and Pastoral Theology, Director of Lay Spiritual Formation, St. Augustine's Seminary

"I am pleased to endorse Caroline Pignat's spiritual guide, *All I Am*. This accessible book for young people is grounded in Scripture, the lives and teachings of the saints, and the foundational truths of our faith about God's goodness and his unconditional love for his creations—me and you! *All I Am* is a wonderful affirmation of the love God has for us and how we can respond in practical ways to the daily effects of his care. It is also an inspiring gift to give to any young person, not only to affirm their identity in God but also to help them discover their purpose as modern missionaries sent to spread the Good News of Jesus Christ in word and action."

MARCEL DAMPHOUSSE, Archbishop of Ottawa-Cornwall

"*All I Am* presents a wonderful journey for young readers seeking to understand life's big questions. Through daily reflections, Caroline shows that it is possible and even essential to have a relationship with God."

TED HURLEY, Coordinator of English Pastoral Services with the Archdiocese of Ottawa-Cornwall

"Caroline Pignat takes the daily trials and tribulations of life and helps the reader realize that God is there for us, so we are never alone. Through prayers, reflections, and Scripture, we see that God wants us to be a messenger for his love. *All I Am* is a must read for teens trying to figure out who they are and where they fit into this world, providing both inspiration and hope for anyone working through the messiness of faith during their developmental years."

TOM D'AMICO, Director of Education, Ottawa Catholic School Board

"In this thought-provoking book of spiritual reflections and prayers, Caroline Pignat invites young readers to think of God as their GPS, acknowledging the challenges of 'adulting' as our youth struggle to find meaning and courage in a world full of uncertainty and angst. With fresh ideas to inspire young people to connect with God through wisdom stories, Scripture, inspirational faith leaders, and saints throughout the ages, she urges teens to develop new images for God that resonate with their lives today. With God as their 'personal trainer,' coaching them through spiritual 'reps' to avoid the pitfalls of click bait, friendship drama, and the shame they carry and the forgiveness they find challenging, Caroline reminds her readers that Jesus walks into the middle of their mess and promises to stay."

MAUREEN DUFOUR, Chaplain, Ottawa Catholic School Board

"Caroline Pignat's mastery as a writer, expertise as an educator, and rich relationship with God have converged in this superb tool for teens. Insightful and practical, *All I Am* invites readers to encounter a close and loving God who shows them the beloved gift of themselves and their lives. This resource helps meet a great need for our teens and our times!"

DR. CAROL KUZMOCHKA, Co-director and Lead Researcher, Centre for Religious Education and Catechesis, and part-time professor, Saint Paul University, Ottawa

"More and more, teens are being tested and pushed to choose their battles, pick a side, stand up for what they believe. But how can anyone choose if they don't yet know what they believe about religion, politics, or social structures? To do that in any meaningful way, we first need to know what we believe about ourselves—who we are and what we want to be. *All I Am* helps readers do just that. By pairing contemplation and prayer with contemporary settings and situations that allow teens to reflect on their world, readers see themselves as God's kids, like him in the ways that really matter—loved, confident, blessed, and gifted."

CAROL BRYDEN, series consultant for Growing in Faith, Growing in Christ

ALL I AM

A CATHOLIC DEVOTIONAL FOR
DISCOVERING WHO YOU ARE IN GOD

CAROLINE PIGNAT

ZONDERVAN®

ZONDERVAN

All I Am
Copyright © 2022 by Caroline Pignat

Requests for information should be addressed to:
Zondervan, *3900 Sparks Dr. SE, Grand Rapids, Michigan 49546*

ISBN 978–0–310–75153–3 (hardcover)
ISBN 978-0-310-14124-2 (audio download)
ISBN 978–0–310–75157–1 (ebook)

Art direction: Cindy Davis
Cover Design: Micah Kandros
Interior Design: Denise Froehlich

Printed in Korea

22 23 24 25 26 / SAM / 10 9 8 7 6 5 4 3 2 1

CONTENTS

WHERE I BELONG

WHO I AM

WHY I AM SAFE

WHAT I CAN DO

WHY I CAN DO IT

INTRODUCTION

Who am I? Where do I belong? What am I good at? Why am I here? Why do I matter?

It's totally normal to have questions like these. But don't worry, no one expects you to know all the answers. Self-discovery is a lifelong adventure. And, good news, you don't have to do it alone. In fact, God doesn't want you to do it alone. He wants to be with you every step of the way.

People may try to answer those questions about themselves in lots of ways, but the truth is, if you really want to know who you are, why you matter, where you belong, and what you can do—ask the One who created you. God can't wait to tell you all about yourself. One way God does that is through his Word. Another is through his Holy Spirit, who is already at work in your life and in your heart. (Maybe that's why you ended up with a copy of this book.)

All I Am helps you better know who you are—by better knowing who God is. For example, if God is loving—that means you are loved. A lot! If God is Father—that makes you God's kid. If God is Creator—that means you're his one-of-a-kind masterpiece. As you dig into each section, you'll discover more truths about God and about yourself.

Ready to start this amazing adventure?

Then make a promise to God and to yourself. For the next ninety days:

- Pray the prayers.
- Read the daily scriptures.

- Think about the reflections.
- Try the journal prompts.

These simple tools will help you dig a little deeper and start to uncover the real, full, and wonderful you. Each section has five days of readings to help you focus on one specific part of your God-given identity. Then, at the end of each section, there's an opportunity to take a day to Rest and Remember—because even God rested on the seventh day. Look back on the things you discovered over the week. Remember what you found. There's no point in finding all that amazing treasure if you just leave it behind and forget about it. That's why journaling helps. It's like digging with power tools.

God knows every wonderful thing about wonderful you—and he can't wait for you to discover it all. Think of this book as a map. Commit to it. Follow it, step by step, day by day, and it will lead you to a great discovery.

WHERE I BELONG

GOD IS LOVING . . . I AM LOVED

Lord,
I believe in you: increase my faith
I trust you: strengthen my trust.
I love you: let me love you more and more.
Amen.

—EXCERPT FROM UNIVERSAL
PRAYER OF POPE CLEMENT XI

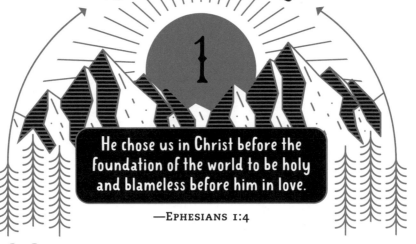

GOD IS LOVING . . . I AM LOVED

1

> He chose us in Christ before the foundation of the world to be holy and blameless before him in love.
>
> —EPHESIANS 1:4

Why am I here? What's my purpose? What's the point of life?

It's no mystery. It's not even a secret. You are here for a reason and that reason is love:

GOD (the all-powerful, all-knowing Creator of the universe)

LOVES (adores, delights in, cherishes, enjoys, and deeply cares for)

YOU (As you are. Right here, right now.)

In fact, he's *crazy* about you! You exist because God loves you. Even before the world began, God *chose* you.

Find that hard to believe? Most of us carry doubts about ourselves because of what experience has taught us. We only have to face rejection a few times to feel unwanted or make a few mistakes to feel incapable. And we believe the hurtful words of others, even if they are blurted in anger.

You can't . . . You'll never . . . You always . . . You're just so . . . Sound familiar? When others make us feel rejected, unloved, or misunderstood, we often take it to heart. We start telling ourselves those lies over and over. It's like having the worst-song-ever looping in our heads. *I'm no good. I don't belong. Nobody really cares about me.*

But the good news is that *none of that is true.* The good news is you can choose the soundtrack of your day and your life. So, what do you want to hear?

If you want to know who you are, why you are, and all you can be—start with the truth: God loves you. Say it, play it over and over until it becomes familiar.

God loves me. GOD loves me. God LOVES me. God loves ME!

Because knowing that—really believing it—changes everything.

When you know how much God is in love with you then you can only live your life radiating that love.

—St. Teresa of Calcutta

God, thank you for loving me. Help me see myself through your eyes and not the opinions of others. Help me to know and become who I really am—the person you made me to be. Amen.

⟫⟫ → Digging Deeper ← ⟪⟪

1. Finish each sentence with a few describing words.
My best friend says I am: _____
My brothers/sisters say I am: _____
My dad/mom says I am: _____
People who don't know me say I am: _____
But I say I am: _____
2. How have others shaped how you see yourself?
3. God deeply loves you, just as you are. How does that make you feel?

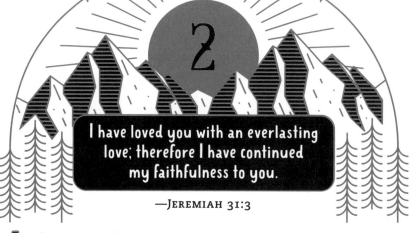

GOD IS LOVING ... I AM LOVED

2

I have loved you with an everlasting love; therefore I have continued my faithfulness to you.

—JEREMIAH 31:3

Look at a snowflake up close and you have to admit, it's pretty amazing. Each is a miniature sculpture of ice and—though there are billions—no two are the same. If a simple snowflake blows your mind, take a closer look at your incredible self. You are a master-planned, well-designed one of a kind! God made you exactly the way you are and loves everything about you.

Wait. Hold up, you say. *God made me like* this *on purpose? With this* [insert disliked feature of choice]? *Gee, thanks.*

We are so familiar with ourselves, we hardly even notice what's amazing. In fact, we look in the mirror and think: *Ugh.* Instead of feeling awe, or wonder, or even gratitude—we complain, usually about some physical feature: *I'm too tall. I'm so short. I'm so fat. I'm too thin. I hate my freckles.* For some reason, we want to look like someone cooler. Someone hotter. Someone stronger. Someone . . . better.

God made you. He loves you as you are. And when you start seeing yourself as he sees you, you'll understand why. That shift in perspective takes time and prayer.

Next time you look in the mirror, look for what is true and good—inside and out. God gave you that amazing body and the life within you. He gave you a heart that beats about one hundred thousand times a day. Lungs that breathe. Senses that see, smell, hear, taste, and feel. Most importantly, he gave you a brain with as many neurons as there are stars in the Milky Way galaxy.

God gave you your one-of-a-kind personality. Those talents and interests. That quirky sense of humor and the great laugh that goes with it. All of those things are what make you, YOU.

> **Before God created anything, he loved. That is what he did: he loved. God always loves.**
>
> —POPE FRANCIS

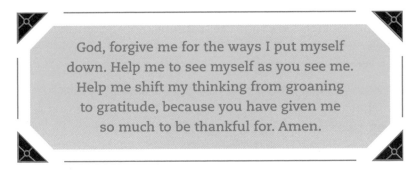

The truth is, we will never see and appreciate all we are if we long to be someone else. We are pretty amazing. God knows it. Maybe it's time to see ourselves through his eyes.

God, forgive me for the ways I put myself down. Help me to see myself as you see me. Help me shift my thinking from groaning to gratitude, because you have given me so much to be thankful for. Amen.

Digging Deeper

1. List five insecurities you have about yourself. Think about who or what made you think that about yourself. Ask yourself: Is it really true?
2. Revision is seeing things with new eyes. Go back and revise each item in your list with a statement that is good and true.

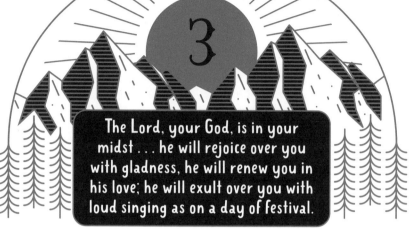

GOD IS LOVING . . . I AM LOVED

3

> The Lord, your God, is in your midst . . . he will rejoice over you with gladness, he will renew you in his love; he will exult over you with loud singing as on a day of festival.
>
> —Zephaniah 3:17–18

Surprise parties are fun. The planning. The decorating. That long wait in the darkened room until we can jump out and yell, "SURPRISE!!!" The best part is the reaction of that special person. It's the moment they realize how much they are loved.

That's how God feels about you. The Bible tells us God wants to celebrate you . . . to **rejoice** and **exult** over you . . . to **delight** in you.[1] Seriously. You are kind of a big deal.

In hundreds of ways, every day, God jumps out and yells, "SURPRISE!"

Don't believe me? Think about it. You know when it feels so good to be in bright sunshine, and the air is so fresh you take a deep breath and sigh? That's him. Or when you're laughing with your friends and don't remember what started it, but everyone is having such a good time together? That's God too. Or when you are having a rough day and your mom somehow knows and gives you a hug? Yep. Those are his arms.

---

1. Go to Psalm 18:19 and Isaiah 62:4–5 to see exactly how God feels about you.

Or maybe it was the moment when time seemed to stop—when you closed your eyes and raised your face to the rain, when you walked in the woods, or sat just looking at the clouds. God especially loves to surprise us through his creation.

The point is, God reaches out all the time. We feel it. We see it. We sense that moment of joy, peace, or love—even if we don't recognize it's him. But whenever we feel deep calm and contentment for no *apparent* reason—God is the reason.

God is having a surprise party for you today. And tomorrow. And every day after for the rest of your life. Remember that. Expect it. Look forward to it. Once we start doing that, we'll notice his decorations, signs, and presence all over. We will see how God is already with us, loving us, celebrating us.

God calls to us in countless little ways all the time.
—St. Teresa of Avila

And God always brings the best gifts!

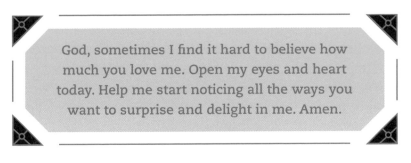

God, sometimes I find it hard to believe how much you love me. Open my eyes and heart today. Help me start noticing all the ways you want to surprise and delight in me. Amen.

Digging Deeper

1. Describe a time you felt totally calm, at peace, or full of joy. Describe it in detail.
2. Where were you? What did you see and hear? How did you feel? Who was with you?
3. Picture God watching that great moment happen. What would he say to you?

> I pray that . . . he may grant that you may be strengthened in your inner being with power through his Spirit, and that Christ may dwell in your hearts through faith, as you are being rooted and grounded in love.

—EPHESIANS 3:16–19

A friendship is like a seed. It starts small at first. Maybe you were on the same team or in the same class, or liked the same bands, or shared that same weird sense of humor nobody else appreciated. Either way, you and your friend clicked, and you've been together ever since. They get you like no one else does. A good friend like this is a real blessing, or as the Bible says, "a treasure" (Sirach 6:14).

Over time, that seed of friendship sprouted and grew deeper roots as you hung out, had fun, and made memories. You were there for each other in difficult times, and when you had problems between you, you worked through it together because the relationship was important. All of this makes your friendship stronger. It makes treasured friendships last, possibly our whole lives.

God loves you—we already covered that—but he really likes you too. He wants to be your treasured friend; a part of your everyday life, there to hang out and make memories. God wants to be there for you in all the ups and downs of your life.

How does a friendship with God work? Where do we even start? Don't worry—God's taken care of that. When he made us, he planted a seed of friendship with him deep inside our hearts. It's ready and waiting to grow into something amazing, beyond what we can even imagine. God also gives us the tools and the help we need to do our part to make it grow.

> **Prayer is nothing else than being on terms of friendship with God.**
> —St. Teresa of Avila

And if he can grow a one-hundred-foot tree from a one-inch acorn—just imagine what he can do for us, and with us, and through us if we just say yes.

God, thank you for always being there for me. Help me to think of you as a constant, treasured friend, someone I can turn to no matter what. I want to do my part to help our friendship grow even stronger. Holy Spirit, please show me how. Amen.

Digging Deeper

Tell God what is on your mind and heart right now. He wants to hear all about it. Speak to him as you would speak to your closest friend.

GOD IS LOVING ... I AM LOVED

5

Draw near to God, and he will draw near to you.

—JAMES 4:8

Ever feel lonely in a crowd, restless, or just unfulfilled? It's like something is missing.

We all hunger for something . . . *more*. Many people chase after the next trend, the perfect look, or the most likes on an online post. Other people try to numb that longing by bingeing on gaming, movies, social media, food, shopping, or alcohol and drugs. But none of these things will ever leave us feeling satisfied, because what we are really craving is God.

We are made to love. To belong. To be in relationship with God and others. God designed us that way. So it isn't surprising that nothing else fills and fulfils us quite like him.

Want to truly fill that deep longing? Draw near to God. It's that simple.

God made the first move when he planted the seed of faith in our hearts. It's what makes us wonder about him. It's what makes us long for him, even if at first we don't realize it is God we need. God sows that seed of faith, he sends that friend request, he gently calls us by name—and he waits.

How we respond is up to each one of us. The truth is, we are as close to God as we want to be.

Our closest relationships are strong because we spend time with those people. We tell them about all the ups and downs of our days. It might be a quick shout out or a long heart-to-heart, but what matters isn't how long we talk, it's how often, as well as how open and present we are. These special people are important in our lives because they are a *part of* our lives. God wants to be a part of our everyday lives too.

> **Our hearts were made for You, O Lord, and they are restless until they rest in you.**
> —ST. AUGUSTINE

Invite God in. Pray—even for just a few minutes—every day. Draw near to God and you will know that God is with you. He is for you. He hears you and he loves you.

> God, I often feel restless and dissatisfied. I didn't realize that was really my longing for you. Help me to remember to turn to you first knowing only you can fill that God-shaped hole. Amen.

Digging Deeper

1. When I'm feeling down, restless, or like something's missing, I usually . . .
2. What are the top three ways you distract yourself?
3. What will you do to ensure you spend time with God—the one we need most?

GOD IS LOVING ... I AM LOVED

6

God is love, and those who abide in love abide in God, and God abides in them.

—1 JOHN 4:16

The Bible is a collection of seventy-three books that took over a thousand years to write. It's rich in history—but it isn't a history book. It describes the creation of the world—but it isn't a science book. It tells people's stories, including key events in Jesus's life—but it isn't a biography. In fact, the Gospels mainly focus on the last three years of Jesus's life. If we had to classify the Bible as a specific genre, we could call it a love letter from God to each one of us. Or a guidebook—an owner's manual— for living our best lives with God.

The Bible is full of stories of real people living real lives. We see them struggle with doubt, fear, and temptation. We see how they respond to God's call. But every person's sacred story is in the Bible to help us live our own story. Their faithfulness and even their failings show us that God is always at work in their lives, which helps us to recognize how that same God is always at work in ours. Like us, these people are not perfect or always faithful—but God is.

As we read about what God says and does for them, we better know who God is for us. God keeps his promises to Abraham and Sarah—and we know **God is faithful**. God reassures Moses for the task ahead—and we know **God is helpful**. God forgives David for his betrayal and lies—and we know **God is merciful**. Those are just three examples. The Bible has thousands more.

If you've tried reading the Bible from page 1, you might have felt a bit lost or overwhelmed. The best place to start is with the Holy Spirit. Ask him to be with you and guide you as you read. He inspired the authors who wrote God's Word. He inspires the Church, who interprets and teaches God's Word. And he longs to inspire you as you read God's Word and apply it to your life.

> God, thank you for the ways you teach me, guide me, reassure me, and love me through your Word. May your Holy Spirit give me understanding and wisdom as I read it. Amen.

1. What's your favorite Bible story or quote? Why?
2. What is God telling your heart through it?

That is why we need His word: So that we can hear, amid the thousands of other words in our daily lives, that one word that speaks to us not about things, but about life.

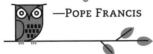

—POPE FRANCIS

GOD IS LOVING ... I AM LOVED

R&R: Rest and Remember

Look back over what you read and wrote this week. What's your main takeaway?

_____

_____

_____

_____

_____

_____

_____

_____

_____

_____

WHERE I BELONG

GOD IS FATHER ... I AM GOD'S CHILD

Gracious and holy Father, grant us the intellect to understand you, reason to discern you, diligence to seek you, wisdom to find you, a spirit to know you, a heart to meditate upon you. Amen.

—TAKEN FROM THE PRAYER OF ST. BENEDICT

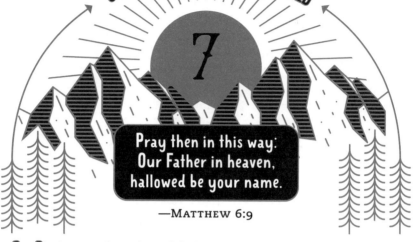

GOD IS FATHER... I AM GOD'S CHILD

7

Pray then in this way:
Our Father in heaven,
hallowed be your name.

—MATTHEW 6:9

Who's your favorite celebrity, athlete, or singer? You really admire this person's talents—you know all their stats and achievements. Clearly, you're their number one fan. So picture how insanely excited you'd be to meet someone who *actually knows* them! Not only that, they've offered to help you meet your hero!

Obviously, it helps to know someone on the inside. And, thankfully, we do.

We've got Jesus.

But Jesus is doing something even better than getting us backstage passes to one concert or VIP seats to the big game. What he's offering is way more than a one-time intro for a quick selfie and signature. Thanks to Jesus, we have eternal, exclusive access to God the Father, an unlimited supply of the Holy Spirit's power, and are able to literally join their family. That's right—God is adopting us.

Think about that for a moment. The God of the universe wants you as his beloved child.

Maybe you have a great dad or a special father figure in your life. Maybe you don't. Either way, God wants to be the

Perfect Dad for you. He wants to care for you and provide for you; to protect you and guide you throughout your life in ways that only he can. Most of all, he wants to fill you with all his loving goodness so that you overflow with joy. Pretty amazing, huh?

It's not something we deserve. It's not even anything we can earn. It's all a gift—God's gift to you. Why? Because God loves you.

God loves you more than anyone ever has—or ever will—and nothing will ever change that. Jesus came to

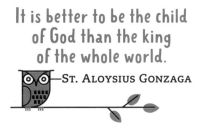

It is better to be the child of God than the king of the whole world.

—St. Aloysius Gonzaga

earth so that we could really get to know his Father—our Father. Jesus invites us into their love. To sit at their table. To become a part of their family and a part of their lives, and to make them a part of ours. That's what it means to be God's kid.

And that's something totally worth cheering about.

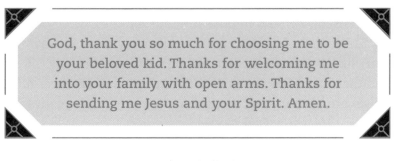

God, thank you so much for choosing me to be your beloved kid. Thanks for welcoming me into your family with open arms. Thanks for sending me Jesus and your Spirit. Amen.

Digging Deeper

1. How does it feel to know you belong in God's family?
2. What blessings and responsibilities come with that belonging?

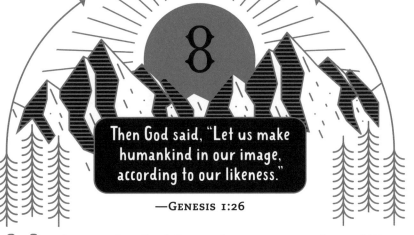

GOD IS FATHER … I AM GOD'S CHILD

8

Then God said, "Let us make humankind in our image, according to our likeness."

—Genesis 1:26

Who do you take after? Do you have your mom's eyes? Her thoughtfulness? Or maybe you take after your dad when it comes to height, humor, and hopefulness. You might even take after your grandparents or some ancestor you've never even met. Be it nature (in our genes) or nurture (in how we were raised), we tend to take after our families.

This can be frustrating if we take after them in ways we don't like. It can also be frustrating for those of us who never had the chance to know our birth parents. But whatever family we are born into or brought up in, thankfully we all take after our Heavenly Dad, God.

We don't have God's skin color, shape, or shoe size. Our Heavenly Dad has none of those things. But God made us in his image. We take after him in ways that really matter: spiritually, intellectually, morally, and relationally. It's who we naturally are.

Look at any two-year-old and you will already see some of God's traits shining through. They create because God creates. They delight because God delights. And so do we. Just like our Heavenly Dad, we want what is good, right, and true—even if we sometimes fail to choose those paths. We think and reason—even if we sometimes make the wrong choices. We are growing in compassion and faithfulness—even if selfishness often lurks nearby. Most of all we long to belong, to be loved, and to love, because God is love. We have all we need within us to take after God. Just imagine how much more these wonderful traits could develop with a little more effort and focus.

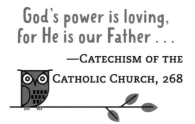

God's power is loving, for He is our Father . . .

—CATECHISM OF THE CATHOLIC CHURCH, 268

God is our Father. But unlike those Greek mythology sagas, that doesn't mean we are gods or even godlike. We are, however, meant to be godly. To take after God, to work at developing his qualities in us. Godliness is both in our nature and takes nurturing.

Thankfully, we have a whole lifetime to follow in his footsteps.

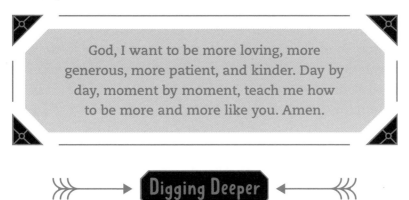

God, I want to be more loving, more generous, more patient, and kinder. Day by day, moment by moment, teach me how to be more and more like you. Amen.

Digging Deeper

1. Are you creative? Loving? Joyful? Patient? What are some ways you are starting to take after your Heavenly Dad?
2. What are some ways you would like to be more like him? Ask him for help.

GOD IS FATHER ... I AM GOD'S CHILD

9

For all who are led by the Spirit of God are children of God.

—ROMANS 8:14

Every person is created by God and loved by God. Following Jesus and the Holy Spirit makes us children of God. That means we aren't just made by God, we don't just believe in God, we actually *belong* to God's family.

We were welcomed into that family through baptism. Our baptism was a pretty incredible milestone in our lives, even if we were too little to remember it. In that moment we became members of the Church, sisters and brothers of Jesus, and children of God. It is the start of our covenant, or promise, with God.

Promises matter. Keeping them strengthens our relationships. It builds trust and loyalty. It shows faithfulness. And we know that no matter how we fail or falter, God never breaks his promises to us.

Baptism is our first official "yes!" to God. We can only receive the rite once, but baptism isn't a one-and-done thing. Our parents or godparents may have said the first promise of yes for us when we were babies, but we keep saying that yes to God each day of our lives as we discover what it means to live out that promise to be his. Every moment of every day, God is proposing to us:

I love you. I always have and always will. I just want to spend every day of your life with you. I want to be there for you in good times and bad. I'm here for you, always, no matter what. I have so many good things planned for you. So many gifts in store. Help build my kingdom on earth and, at the end of your life, I promise you we will spend forever together in heaven.

A wedding ceremony is just the beginning of a marriage. In the same way, our baptism is the beginning of a wonderful, loving, committed relationship with the Father, Son, and Holy Spirit. We have our whole lives to live out the loving promises we made together with God, together with the Church, and together as one body of Christ.

He who believes in Christ becomes a son of God.

—Catechism of the Catholic Church, 1709

God, thank you for welcoming me into your family. Help me keep my promises to you. Open my eyes to the ways I can say "yes!" to you today. Amen.

Digging Deeper

What promise are you making to God at this time in your life?

10

As God's chosen ones, holy and beloved, clothe yourselves with compassion, kindness, humility, meekness, and patience ... forgive each other; just as the Lord has forgiven you ... Above all, clothe yourselves with love, which binds everything together in perfect harmony.

—COLOSSIANS 3:12–14

Baptism calls us to be Christlike. But how are we answering? We want to do the right thing, *but* . . . We don't plan to lose our temper, *but* . . . We don't mean to be cruel, *but* . . .

She started it. He had it coming. They were driving me nuts.

It's so easy to blame everyone else for how we are acting. People lie to us. Gossip about us. Betray our trust. When our world seems unfair, ugly, and unkind, it's not surprising that we fall short and react in ways and words that are anything but Christlike.

It's not surprising—but it's not right. It can be hard to be patient and kind like Jesus. It's difficult to forgive and forget. We fail and fall often. God, our loving Father, understands and doesn't love us any less when we fall short. But he does expect us to keep at it. He helps us up. He dusts us off. And he gently whispers, *Try again.*

It's like learning to ride a bike. The steps were clear. Making it happen was another story. The process was hard: hard enough to make us want to give up. But we didn't. We persevered because what we wanted was worth the effort. Every little improvement gave us hope. It made us try again and again. Even though we fell off more times than we liked, we never gave up, and—eventually—made it all the way around the block.

I pray that each one of you be holy and so spread his love everywhere you go.

—St. Teresa of Calcutta

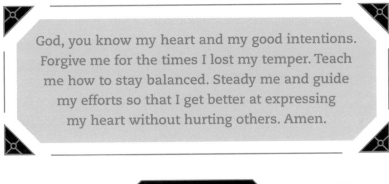

In the same way, becoming Christlike takes commitment and effort. It means practicing compassion and kindness. It means working at being patient and forgiving. It means noticing and celebrating the ways we are growing more loving and kinder. Sure, there will be times we slip and fall, but with God's help, we get right back up and begin again.

Because love is always worth it.

> God, you know my heart and my good intentions. Forgive me for the times I lost my temper. Teach me how to stay balanced. Steady me and guide my efforts so that I get better at expressing my heart without hurting others. Amen.

Digging Deeper

1. Write about a situation that is really frustrating you.
2. What did you do right? What might you have done wrong?
3. If you think of it like learning to ride a bike, what lessons can you learn from this experience? Ask God for help.

GOD IS FATHER ... I AM GOD'S CHILD

11

You shall love the Lord your God with all your heart, and with all your soul, and with all your mind, and with all your strength.

—MARK 12:30

Is it okay to feel angry at God?

Good question. God wants us to share our whole hearts and minds when we speak to him—so don't hold anything back. Even anger. God doesn't want us to shrug and say, "I'm fine" if we are not. He doesn't want us to pretend or, worst of all, to avoid him altogether.

God already knows what's going on in our lives. He knows our struggles and our worries. He understands our frustration and grief—and he's just waiting for us to turn to him for help.

In those low moments, when we don't understand why things happened, we can wonder, *Where is God in all of this?* We might even feel angry with God. Anger is a normal human emotion. What we do with that anger is what matters most.

So vent, rant, or cry—but take your hurting heart to God and let him help you. Because he will. No matter what caused the pain, God wants to hold you through it. He wants to be with you in it. Above all, he wants to heal you of it.

In David's numerous psalms we see his joy and gratitude, his doubt and fears, his shame and regrets. And, sometimes, even his anger. In Psalm 13:1–2, David rants, "Will you forget me forever? How long will you hide your face from me? How long must I bear pain in my soul and have sorrow in my heart all day long?"

Clearly, this guy is really upset with God. David's words are challenging, raw, real, and angry. But most importantly, they are prayers. He is telling God all about how he

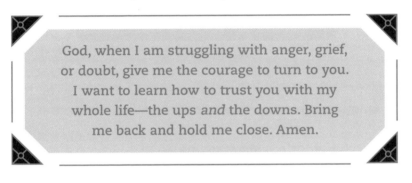

A quarrel between friends, when made up, adds a new tie to friendship.

—St. Francis de Sales

feels. And at the end, David has a sense of hope. He trusts.[1] He rejoices.[2] Because he knows God always hears and always answers our prayers.

Often in the ways we least expect.

God, when I am struggling with anger, grief, or doubt, give me the courage to turn to you. I want to learn how to trust you with my whole life—the ups *and* the downs. Bring me back and hold me close. Amen.

Digging Deeper

Confused? Annoyed? Frustrated with God about something? Try expressing it with your own psalm.

- Start by focusing on yourself: tell God exactly how you feel and why.
- End by focusing on God: remember who he is, how he loves, and what he can do.

1. See Psalm 13:5
2. See Psalm 13:6

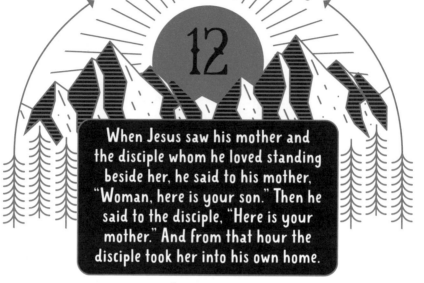

GOD IS FATHER...I AM GOD'S CHILD

12

> When Jesus saw his mother and the disciple whom he loved standing beside her, he said to his mother, "Woman, here is your son." Then he said to the disciple, "Here is your mother." And from that hour the disciple took her into his own home.

—JOHN 19:25–27

Mary was specially chosen by God the Father to be the mother of his Son, Jesus. She was only a teenager at the time, yet we see how her faith and obedience to God didn't depend on her own understanding.

When the angel Gabriel appeared to her, Mary must have been afraid and confused. She didn't understand God's plan, but she never doubted what she was told. Instead, she trusted God and said *yes*.

Mary was the first disciple. She was the first to believe in Jesus—God's Son and our Savior—even before he was born. But Mary's life is more than a biblical story of faith because Mary is still with us today.

Before Jesus died on the cross, he told his disciple John, "Here is your mother." In that moment, Jesus made Mary the mother of John, the mother of the Church, and the Spiritual Mother of each one of us.

Like any loving mother, Mary watches over us. She guides and protects us. She prays for us and with us, if we ask. More than anything, Mary wants to help each of us to better know and love her Son, Jesus, because it is how we can better know and love God the Father. That is why for generations, countless saints, popes, and holy men and women have entrusted themselves to Mary's care. She guided and helped them to grow in holiness—and she can do the same for us. When we pray the rosary, or a Hail Mary, it's as if Mary gently takes us by the hand and leads us closer to Jesus.

We love and honor Mary, but we don't worship her. Our worship is meant for God alone. Instead, we recognize and celebrate Mary's importance in God's plan, in Jesus's heart, and in our lives today.

Never be afraid of loving the Blessed Virgin too much. You can never love her more than Jesus did.

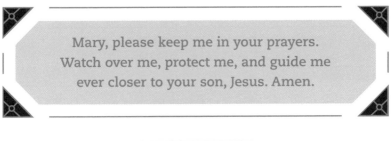 —St. Maximilian Kolbe

Through the example, help, and prayers of our Holy Mother, we come to know God more and more.

> Mary, please keep me in your prayers. Watch over me, protect me, and guide me ever closer to your son, Jesus. Amen.

 **Digging Deeper**

Mary is known for her great faith and humble heart because she completely trusts God and relies on his wisdom and strength.

1. What is something you are struggling to figure out, control, or deal with in your life?
2. What you can learn from Mary's humble example of faith?

GOD IS FATHER... I AM GOD'S CHILD

R&R: Rest and Remember

Look back over what you read and wrote this week. What's your main takeaway?

_____

_____

_____

_____

_____

_____

_____

_____

_____

_____

WHERE I BELONG

GOD IS LOVE . . . I AM LOVING

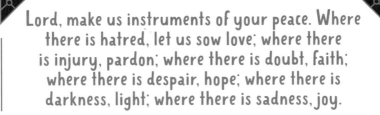

Lord, make us instruments of your peace. Where there is hatred, let us sow love; where there is injury, pardon; where there is doubt, faith; where there is despair, hope; where there is darkness, light; where there is sadness, joy.

—ST. FRANCIS OF ASSISI

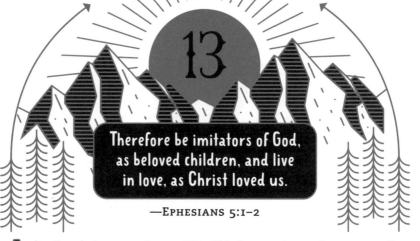

GOD IS LOVE... I AM LOVING

13

Therefore be imitators of God, as beloved children, and live in love, as Christ loved us.

—EPHESIANS 5:1–2

Imitation is how we learn. We didn't even know how to walk or talk until someone showed us. But once we saw them doing it, we wanted to do it too. We imitated them, with actual baby steps, until we figured how do it ourselves. And look at us run now!

As we grew up, we played in our capes and crowns and imitated our favorite cartoon characters. Even today, we still imitate people we admire. We sing like our favorite music artist. We shoot hoops like our favorite baller. We wear the jersey of our favorite team—because they're the best, *obviously*.

But if we want to be more loving, the best person to imitate and learn from is God. Our first baby step in being more loving is to notice some of the countless ways God loves us. We hear it in words. We feel it in his presence and his faithfulness because God never lets us down. We see God's love in his many gifts—just look at the world around us, the family beside us, and the life within us. God is one generous giver.

And even when we make mistakes, God is eager to forgive if we just ask. He doesn't hold a grudge or keep bringing it up. Why? Because he loves us.

So let's take after God and follow in his footsteps. Step by step—in our words and actions, in our presence and support, and by being generous and forgiving with others—let's imitate God's ways and try to love like he loves.

God, the world is full of signs of your love. Open my eyes to see them. Open my ears to hear them. Open my heart and mind to know how much you love me. Teach me to love like you do. Amen.

Digging Deeper

What signs—big and small—in your life show God's love?

You learn to speak by speaking, to study by studying, to run by running, to work by working, and just so, you learn to love God and man by loving.

—St. Frances de Sales

GOD IS LOVE... I AM LOVING

14

Do not love the world or the things in the world.

—1 JOHN 2:15

If we got the latest smartphone, would we use it as a drink coaster? Would we hammer a nail with it? What about using it as a hockey puck? Not likely. No doubt our parents would take it away if they saw us misusing something that valuable. Those phones are super expensive. Probably because they can do amazing things like take photos, text, video chat, run countless apps, surf the net, and play music. That's what a smartphone is designed for. Using it as a coaster, a hammer, or a puck would be a total waste of its potential and purpose.

In the same way, we should be doing what we were made for. Do you know what that is? (Here's a hint: reread the title on this page.)

Love—that's what we're made for! It's our basic design, our deepest need, and our greater purpose. It's who we are, and it's meant to drive why we do what we do. So when we feel lonely, directionless, or just plain off—it's probably a sign to stop wasting our God-given potential and start doing more of what we're made for.

Love is the greatest treasure God gives us—and it only grows more valuable the more we pass it on. But it's important to be aware of how and where we invest that treasure. We've all said, *I love that movie! I love that color! I love this playlist! I love mint-chocolate ice cream!*

Apparently, we love a lot of things. And yes, they are pretty great—especially the ice cream. But that feeling of awe and reverence and that deep tenderness and affection coming from our heart is meant for others. Not things. Loving things will never make us feel whole, satisfied, or truly happy—only relationships can. And only a relationship with God can do it fully.

We become what we love and who we love shapes what we become.

—St. Clare of Assisi

God designed us to love him and to love one another. Why waste yourself on anything less?

> God, I give my time and attention to many things that don't deserve my heart. Help me to focus more on the people in my life. Help me to start noticing the blessings that they are, to be grateful for the love they give me, and to be eager to show love in return. Amen.

Digging Deeper

1. List your top five relationships.
2. Beside each name, write one or two things you love and admire more about this person. What about them makes you happy and thankful that they are in your life?
3. Now write how you can show them that you care. What's something specific you could do for each one of them? (It doesn't have to be big or complicated. Sometimes the smallest acts of love are the most meaningful.)

GOD IS LOVE... I AM LOVING

15

Little children, let us love, not in word or speech, but in truth and action.

—1 JOHN 3:18

It totally figures that your turn to do the dishes falls on the day your dad made his famous homemade lasagna. He's an enthusiastic chef, which means by the time dinner is done, the kitchen is a total disaster; sauce is everywhere and every pot and plate is dirty. As you stand at the sink, you just know it will take forever to clean everything up.

"Hey, I'll help," your brother says, still sitting at the table. But by your third trip clearing plates, he still hasn't moved.

"Dad," he brags, "don't worry about cleaning up—we got it covered. This kitchen will be spotless."

"Great." Your dad smiles and pats your brother on the back. "You're so awesome for helping out."

Only he isn't. Because *you're* doing it all. Cue the meltdown.

It seems ridiculous for someone to say they're going to help and then not do anything. It's even worse when they are clearly bragging in order to be praised and admired. But this kind of thing happens a lot. And sometimes even we are guilty of it.

We say, *I'll be there for you* . . . but get busy with our own stuff and forget. We say, *You can trust me* . . . but we speak behind their backs. We say, *That joke's mean* . . . but we laugh and pass it on. We say, *I forgive you* . . . but we keep bringing it up to make them feel bad.

It happens every time we say, *I love you* . . . and then act in selfish ways. Our actions will always speak louder than our words. It's easy to say, *I'll help, I'll be there, I forgive you,* or *I love you,* but they are all empty promises if we don't follow through.

Integrity means our actions align with our values. It means keeping our promises, holding our tongues, or serving one another. In big things and small, our actions are what really show love.

God, I know I've let down some of the people I care about. Help me to follow through on what I promise. Give me the strength so my actions let others know how much they really mean to me. Amen.

 **Digging Deeper**

1. Write about a time when you let someone down. How did it make them feel? How does it make you feel?
2. It's never too late to make things right. What will you do to take that first step?

It is so easy to be proud, harsh, moody, and selfish, but we have been created for greater things. Why stoop down to things that will spoil the beauty of our hearts?

 —St. Teresa of Calcutta

GOD IS LOVE... I AM LOVING

16

Just as I have loved you, you also should love one another. By this everyone will know that you are my disciples, if you have love for one another.

—JOHN 13:34–35

After he called his twelve disciples, Jesus spent three years training, teaching, and preparing them. By his example and actions, Jesus showed them how to pray, how to preach, and how to serve. He got them ready to continue his work, to spread the Good News, and to build his Church.

But Jesus had no time for hypocrites. We often read about him calling out and telling off people who were faking holiness and thinking they were better than everyone else. These people were more concerned with looking good than being good. Jesus knew their hearts. He knew they cared more about getting praised than praising God. It sickened him because they were completely missing the point and misleading others as well.

So Jesus made it clear and simple for everyone. He boiled all of his teachings down to just one thing: If you want to be holy, if you want to please God, if you want to be his disciple, **love**.

That's it. That's all. Because, really, that's everything.

Jesus loved. We see it in his every encounter throughout the Gospels. Jesus welcomed everyone equally. He gave abundantly. He served humbly. And he often went out of his way to be with the one person everyone else avoided—because he loved relentlessly.

Being a Christian two thousand years ago, today, or two thousand years from now will always mean being loving. Because that's who Jesus was. It's who he is.

And it's who he calls us to be.

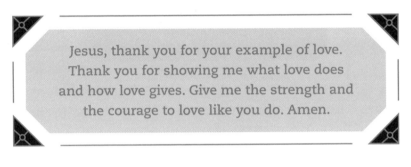

Jesus, thank you for your example of love. Thank you for showing me what love does and how love gives. Give me the strength and the courage to love like you do. Amen.

Digging Deeper

1. Who is usually avoided or ignored by others in your class or school?
2. What is one way you can reach out to them like Jesus would?
3. What will you do this week to help them feel like they matter?

You know well enough that Our Lord does not look so much at the greatness of our actions, nor even at their difficulty, but at the love with which we do them.

—St. Therese of Lisieux

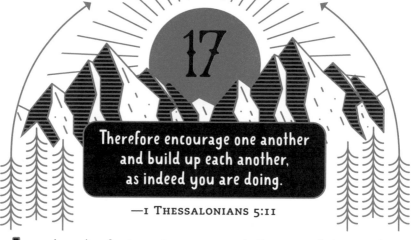

GOD IS LOVE ... I AM LOVING

17

Therefore encourage one another
and build up each another,
as indeed you are doing.

—1 Thessalonians 5:11

Love is a simple, two-step process: 1. See a need, 2. Meet it.

The thing is, most of us are so concerned with *our* wants that we don't pay much attention to the needs of others. While there are some people who will come right out and tell us what they need or even ask for help, most of the time, it's up to us to pick up the clues.

For example, if a friend seems unusually quiet—something is bothering them. Just stopping, noticing, and asking, *What's up? You doing okay?* might be the loving thing to do.

Other times, people's needs are expressed in ways that annoy us. Little kids whine when they need attention. Adults get short-tempered when they need a break from the demands of adulting. Our best friend might even say something hurtful if they've felt ignored by us lately.

It's so easy to react by yelling back, sulking, or stomping off. We just want to get away from them. But doing the loving thing means stopping and seeing. Seeing past our reactions, seeing beyond their behaviors, and seeing into their hearts. Ask the Holy Spirit for the wisdom to understand why this person is acting this way: *What's going on with them right now? What do they need?* Then ask the Holy Spirit, *How can I help?*

The Holy Spirit loves to inspire us. Ideas will start popping into our heads:

My brother's bored. I could . . . play a game with him.
Mom's stressed. I could . . . help with dinner.
My friend's down. I could . . . invite him on a bike ride.

Those simple, small acts—such little efforts on our part—make a huge difference for someone else. That's what love is. That's what love does.

Remember that nothing is small in the eyes of God. Do all that you do with love.

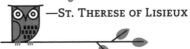 —St. Therese of Lisieux

God wants us to be loving. He wants to love others through us. When we focus less on ourselves and more on others, when we ask for God's help, we will find tons of ways to do that loving thing.

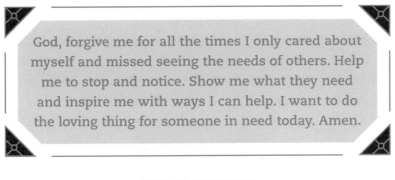

God, forgive me for all the times I only cared about myself and missed seeing the needs of others. Help me to stop and notice. Show me what they need and inspire me with ways I can help. I want to do the loving thing for someone in need today. Amen.

Digging Deeper

1. Who has been irritating you lately? Try writing about things from *their* point of view. What might be going on with them? What might be something they need?
2. Now come up with one simple thing you can do to reach out and help them this week.

GOD IS LOVE... I AM LOVING

18

We love because he first loved us.

—1 John 4:19

A baby doesn't have the words or understanding to describe what love is—but that doesn't mean she doesn't know love. She experiences it every time her mother's voice soothes her. Every time her father's arms hold her. She knows what it means to be cared for, safe, fed, comforted, and held close— she feels love, even if she can't explain it.

But love doesn't exist in isolation. Like a gift, it needs both a giver and a receiver. That is why we are made to belong. We are made to be in relationship with God and others because that is the only way we can give and receive love.

The Holy Trinity is the perfect example of that loving relationship. The love between the Father and Jesus is the power of the Holy Spirit. That means we know how to give and receive love the more we come to know God—and we know God the more we open ourselves to love.

Confused? Don't worry. Saints and theologians have pondered this mystery for generations. It's beyond what our brains can understand. But just because we can't explain it, that doesn't make it untrue. That's where faith comes in.

God gives us faith to truly believe that God is love. That God loves us. And that God's love lives in us to be shared through us to others. Even if we can't explain it, like that baby we know what it is to be cared for, safe, fed, comforted, and held close by God. Because of that, we know how to receive and how to give love. Our loving God designed us that way.

> God, thank you for loving me and teaching me how to love. I can't grasp it in my head, but I feel it in my heart. Give me the faith to receive that gift and the generosity to pass it on. Amen.

Digging Deeper

We first know God's love through the people who love us.
1. Describe a time when someone made you feel cared for, comforted, and loved.
2. Thank God for those special people who taught you how to love.

> Wherever there is love, there is a Trinity: a lover, a beloved, and a fountain of love.
> —St. Augustine

GOD IS LOVE... I AM LOVING

R&R: Rest and Remember

Look back over what you read and wrote this week. What's your main takeaway?

_____

_____

_____

_____

_____

_____

_____

_____

_____

_____

_____

WHO I AM

GOD IS CREATOR . . . I AM GOD'S MASTERPIECE

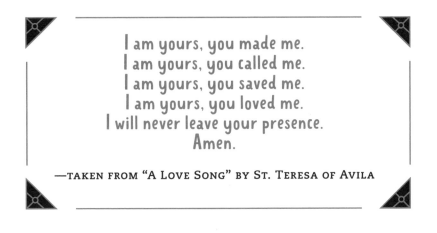

I am yours, you made me.
I am yours, you called me.
I am yours, you saved me.
I am yours, you loved me.
I will never leave your presence.
Amen.

—TAKEN FROM "A LOVE SONG" BY ST. TERESA OF AVILA

GOD IS CREATOR ... I AM GOD'S MASTERPIECE

19

The heavens are telling the glory of God; and the firmament proclaims his handiwork.

—PSALM 19:1

Nature fascinated us when we were little. Remember crouching to watch a trail of ants, discovering that bee buzzing in and out of blossoms to gather pollen and nectar, or feeling that caterpillar rippling along your hand?

As we grew, so did that curiosity and awe. We loved learning fascinating facts about the natural world and sharing it with anyone who'd listen.

God made our minds curious on purpose. He designed us to explore and discover, to be hungry to learn and know. It's one way we understand the world and our place in it. It makes us faithful stewards of creation—because as we understand the needs of different species and environments, we can make sure our choices are helping instead of hurting our world.

But as we mature, we can often lose our kidlike sense of wonder. Our amazing discoveries haven't changed. But, somehow, we have. For whatever reason, we don't see anything all that interesting in another spiderweb, another rock, or another sunset. We don't bother looking up at the moon or down at a dandelion because we think, *I've seen it all before.* It's so familiar, we think we "already know" and so we no longer take notice or take care.

One of the best ways to reconnect with God—and with our sense of awe—is through the world he has made. So get outside. Get dirty. Get lost in the wonderful world just waiting in your own backyard. Pay attention because there is always more to see, and smell, and savor. God waits to meet us, restore us, inspire us, and delight us through his amazing creation.

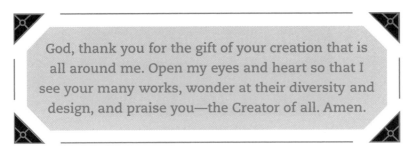

God, thank you for the gift of your creation that is all around me. Open my eyes and heart so that I see your many works, wonder at their diversity and design, and praise you—the Creator of all. Amen.

Digging Deeper

1. What part of nature fascinated you when you were a kid? Spend time digging a little deeper in that subject. Go to the nature museum, research online, or just get outside. What do your discoveries tell you about God?
2. What does it mean to you to be a steward of creation? What's one thing you will start doing to help care for God's world?

Every day, my love for the mountains grows more and more. If my studies permitted, I'd spend whole days in the mountains contemplating the Creator's greatness in that pure air.

—BLESSED PIER GIORGIO FRASSATI

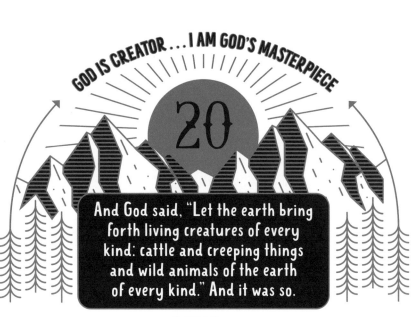

GOD IS CREATOR ... I AM GOD'S MASTERPIECE

20

And God said, "Let the earth bring forth living creatures of every kind: cattle and creeping things and wild animals of the earth of every kind." And it was so.

—GENESIS 1:24

Genesis is not a biology textbook. It doesn't give the steps of creation like we'd describe a frog's lifecycle. In fact, there are *two* accounts of creation, each with a different focus.

Right now, you're probably asking, *Okay . . . so what is true?*

All of it. It's all God's Word, and God does not lie. Ever. The creation story is not meant to be read *literally*—but that doesn't mean it isn't true. It's a sacred story that teaches deep truths about *who* God is, *what* he made, and *why* he made it.

Genesis tells us God created the world and everything in it. The entire earth—every plant and creature—is all God's inspiration, plan, and handiwork. Every part of God's creation is unique and necessary. Including you.

Each creature, plant, and organism is specifically created to thrive in the web of life. These diverse creatures, plants, and organisms interact and depend on each other for survival. From the vast biome of the rainforest to the micro ecosystem hidden under a rotten log, every environment is a unique example of the diversity and connectedness of creation.

The more we become aware of nature and God's master plan, the more we appreciate his many masterpieces, including ourselves. Nothing is accidental or random. That is what Genesis wants us to know. It's what God wants us to know.

In those moments of connection—when we feel peace camping beneath the stars or awe in a thunderstorm—we are reminded of the One who made them all. Those moments of wonder become prayer. Moments of praise. And little by little, we draw closer to the One who made us all.

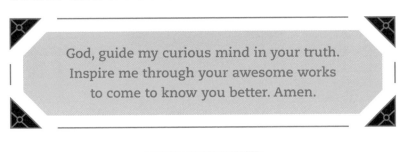

God, guide my curious mind in your truth. Inspire me through your awesome works to come to know you better. Amen.

Digging Deeper

1. Consider this: God wants us to know that all of creation is made *on purpose* and *for a purpose*. And so are you. How does that realization make you feel?
2. Recall a time and place where you most felt connected to the Creator. Capture and save that holy memory in your journal—you can even use a photo, poem, or illustration.

When I was six or seven years old I saw the sea for the first time. The sight made a deep impression on me, I could not take my eyes off it. Its majesty, and the roar of the waves, all spoke to my soul of the greatness and power of God.
—St. Thérèse of Lisieux

GOD IS CREATOR . . . I AM GOD'S MASTERPIECE

21

And God saw that
it was good.

—GENESIS 1:25

It feels good to do a great job, like getting through a tough workout, completing a work of art, or finishing that 1,000-piece puzzle. After all your effort, it feels great to sit back and admire your work. To smile to yourself and think, *Hey, that turned out pretty good!*

We take after God in that. He does the same thing when he creates. In Genesis, we read that God created light and saw that it was good. He separated land from sea and saw that it was good. And at each stage—whether God was creating plants, the moon and stars, or every living creature of land, sea, and air—we read that God saw that it was good.

Yeah, we get it. It's all good. So why the repetition? Well, for one thing, God is showing us over and over that it's good to stop and appreciate what is good. God even takes a rest from good work on day seven and wants us to do the same. Stopping and noticing what is good in the world and in our everyday lives makes us thankful. It makes us hopeful. It gives us peace. All good things.

But more than that, Genesis is showing us that God is good. Everything God makes is good—and that includes you.

You may not feel good. Especially when others judge you and cut you down with their words or actions, or you criticize yourself. At times like that, it's hard to believe you're any good at all. But the truth is: You. Are. Good. You always were and you always will be because God made you that way. Mistakes don't change that. Opinions don't change that. There is nothing anyone can say or do that changes what you are at the core.

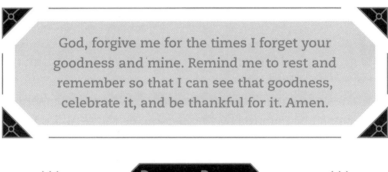

Each of us is the result of a thought of God. Each of us willed, each of us loved, each of us is necessary.

—Pope Benedict XVI

God, forgive me for the times I forget your goodness and mine. Remind me to rest and remember so that I can see that goodness, celebrate it, and be thankful for it. Amen.

Digging Deeper

Does your Sunday seem like every other day of the week? What are some ways you can rest and remember God's goodness and presence in your life?

GOD IS CREATOR ... I AM GOD'S MASTERPIECE

22

Yet, O Lord, you are our Father; we are the clay, and you are our potter; we are all the work of your hand.

—ISAIAH 64:8

Whether they're famous or not, the world is full of amazing people doing amazing things. It's good to admire the greatness in others, though we may sometimes feel a twinge of jealousy or envy their achievements. When those feelings rise, instead be inspired by that person. Be thankful for them. Noticing how someone else shines and thrives often encourages us to do the same.

Many times in that process of being inspired, it's natural to try to become like the people we admire. We model ourselves after them. But no matter how their influence shapes us, we are not meant to become a duplicate. Imagine if every artist just tried to copy *Mona Lisa*. The world of art would be pretty limited and boring. Or imagine if every musician only did Elvis covers. We'd miss out on having other great songs and different genres in our playlists. It's good to be inspired, but it's also important to be original and true to ourselves. It's important to stay open to God's inspiration too.

Each one of us is God's one-of-a-kind work of art, made from the millions of unique things that make us, us. Our humor and personalities; our talents and interests; our way of seeing and being (even our odd quirks)—they are all part of God's plan. If we let God shape and mold us, like clay on a pottery wheel, he will spend our lives forming us into the masterpieces he has in mind. Only God knows what that looks like. And only he can help us become what we're meant to be.

So celebrate all that is good and creative. It all comes from our Good Creator. Be inspired by the beautiful gifts and achievements of others. And be open to God's plan for you. You're an original. And the world needs what makes you, you.

God, you are an amazing creator. Help me to trust in your plan for me. Help me to accept those parts of myself that I don't like. Show me the beauty in all that you have made, including myself. Amen.

Digging Deeper

1. What makes you different from your family and friends?
2. How do you think God can use those differences for good?

> A rough and unshapen log has no idea that it can be made into a statue that will be considered a masterpiece, but the carver sees what can be done with it. So many . . . do not understand that God can mold them into saints, until they put themselves into the hands of that almighty Artisan.
>
> —St. Ignatius of Loyola

GOD IS CREATOR... I AM GOD'S MASTERPIECE

23

Do you not know that you are God's temple and that God's Spirit dwells in you?

—I Corinthians 3:16

King Solomon knew the importance of creating a special dwelling place for God. Built around 957 BCE, Solomon's Temple took over 180,000 artisans, two billion dollars' worth of gold and silver, and seven years to create. It was a temple to house God's presence in the inner room, the Holy of Holies. Today, however, God's Spirit lives in the hearts of those who believe in him. He lives in us. Thanks to Jesus and the Holy Spirit, we are God's temples.

Think about that for a second: *God lives in you and me.* Actually, that's worth thinking about more deeply because we forget that amazing truth. Or so it seems. We live in ways that are anything but reverent and holy. We fill our heads and hearts with things that disrespect God and his will. As Sister Joan Chittister wrote, "We forget the presence of God, and so act as if God were not present."[1] Can you relate?

Being God's temple makes us caretakers of God's home. That means keeping our bodies healthy by getting enough rest, exercise, and eating right. It means cleaning out the garbage and protecting that sacred space. In a way, it also makes us

1. *Wisdom Distilled from the Daily* (HarperCollins, 1991), p. 58.

bouncers who guard the door and turn away those unwelcome thoughts that like to wander in and vandalize our minds and hearts. Lastly, being God's temple means that unlike Solomon's stationary building, we bring God with us wherever we go. Every place. Every encounter. We're God's ride.

But the best part of being God's temple is that God is with us. Always. He's as close and life-giving as our very breath. In Solomon's Temple, only the high priest could enter the Holy of Holies, and that was just one day a year. But thanks to Jesus and the Holy Spirit, we can quiet ourselves and meet God in our hearts any time and all the time.

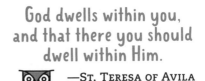

God dwells within you, and that there you should dwell within Him.

—St. Teresa of Avila

Make time. Enter the space for a heart-to-heart or even a quick hello. God's waiting inside.

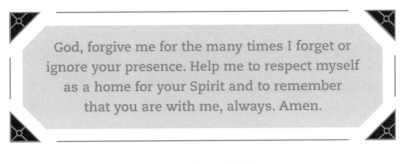

God, forgive me for the many times I forget or ignore your presence. Help me to respect myself as a home for your Spirit and to remember that you are with me, always. Amen.

Digging Deeper

1. Do you ever feel overrun by fearful, anxious, or lustful thoughts that seem to barge in and destroy your peace? How does it feel to try to handle these things on your own?
2. Now tell God about what's troubling you. Ask and he will give you the strength to kick those thoughts to the curb. He wants to help you protect that sacred space inside of you.

GOD IS CREATOR . . . I AM GOD'S MASTERPIECE

24

See what love the Father has given us, that we should be called children of God; and that is what we are.

—1 John 3:1

It's pretty mind-blowing to realize we're God's works of art. Just think about it:

- *God made you in his image.*
- *You're his original masterpiece.*
- *You're God's kid and you take after him.*
- *You are good because God is good.*
- *You love because God is love.*

It might take some time and prayer for all that to sink in. It can be hard to believe that we are God's beloved masterpiece. It's harder still to believe it about other people.

You know who I'm talking about. We might feel tempted to judge them for the way they act or the things they say. Especially if what they have done has affected us personally. But that guy who's so annoying, that girl who is always mean, that grumpy neighbor, even that bully at school—*they're* all God's masterpieces too. He loves them just as deeply. They matter just as much to God. In fact, *every* human on the planet matters to God. And because of that, they matter to us.

Each of us have human dignity. It's a part of who we are—because of *whose* we are. Being treated with respect and compassion is everyone's God-given right simply because God created us. Like a masterpiece painting, we are highly valued and treasured because of the master that made us.

It doesn't matter how old or young we are; it isn't dependent on what we can do, what we have, or where we live. And it isn't just for

My humanity is bound up in yours, for we can only be human together.

—DESMOND TUTU

those who believe. God calls us to ensure that every person's rights are upheld and lived out in our homes, schools, communities, countries, and around the world. It's why we stand in solidarity, it's why we care for the poor and vulnerable, and it's why we oppose all injustice and promote the common good.

God, forgive me for the times when I've failed to see the goodness and dignity of others. May my words and actions always be rooted in your love. Amen.

Digging Deeper

1. Think of someone you find challenging or irritating. What small thing can you do to treat them with the respect they deserve as God's kid?
2. What injustice in your community, country, or world touches your heart?
3. Raise funds. Raise awareness. Be a voice for change. Even the smallest step makes a difference when we all do our part. What can you do to help others know God's love?

GOD IS CREATOR . . . I AM GOD'S MASTERPIECE

R&R: Rest and Remember

Look back over what you read and wrote this week. What's your main takeaway?

_____

_____

_____

_____

_____

_____

_____

_____

_____

_____

_____

WHO I AM

GOD IS TENDING . . . I AM GROWING

Lord, enlighten my understanding, strengthen my will, purify my heart, and make me holy. Help me repent of my past sins and resist temptation in the future. Help to rise above my human weaknesses and to grow stronger as a Christian. Amen.

—Excerpt from the Universal Prayer of Pope Clement XI

> I am the vine, you are the branches.
> Those who abide in me and I in them
> bear much fruit, because apart
> from me you can do nothing.

—JOHN 15:5

If you nurture a plant by giving it just enough light, water, and warmth, it will grow a little stronger, more rooted and stable, and lusher each day. It's pretty cool to watch it change from sprout to stalk and stem, as leaf by leaf it blossoms into what it's made to be. All from one tiny seed.

Faith is like that. God planted a seed of faith in us and he'll help it grow into something wonderful. The thing is, we want results now. If we exercise, we expect to be stronger. In the same way, if we pray, we expect to be more happy, hopeful, and holy right now. When that doesn't happen, we can get discouraged. Especially if we see God working in and through someone else's life. We might doubt and ask, *Is God listening? Does he even care? Am I doing it right? Does any of this Church stuff make a difference?*

The answer to everything is yes. God listens—always. God cares—deeply. And our simply wanting to be with him, know him, and connect with him is enough because God always comes and meets us where we're at. All of this helps our faith grow. God gave us the Church to be like a trellis that supports us as we grow into the person we are made to be.

Growing in faith is a life-long process that takes time, effort, patience, and daily attention. And especially in those early stages, it takes trust that growth is happening. Deep in our hearts, that little seed of faith is germinating and taking root. God is already at work watering, weeding, and waking up our seed. Every time we turn to him, we work with him as he tends to that sprout of faith, helping it grow a little bit more.

> God, thank you for my seed of faith. Give me the awareness and commitment I need to help it grow. Give me the patience to wait on you and trust in you in this season of my life so that I can become even more fruitful. Amen.

Digging Deeper

Each time we encounter Scripture we see it with new eyes. God speaks through his Word when we open our hearts to him.

1. Ask the Holy Spirit to be with you, and then read John 15:1–17 out loud. (Reading aloud helps us pay attention because we are seeing it and hearing it.) Now write down the phrase that stood out to you. It might even be one word.

2. What do you think God wants you to know? How does this message from Scripture apply to your life right now?

The splendor of the rose and the whiteness of the lily do not rob the little violet of its scent nor the daisy of its simple charm ... If every tiny flower wanted to be a rose, spring would lose its loveliness.

—St. Thérèse of Lisieux

26

> The spirit of God has made me, and the breath of the Almighty gives me life.
>
> —JOB 33:4

God's brushstrokes are everywhere, especially in nature. And once we start paying attention—once we start to notice, explore, and enjoy God's amazing creation—we feel awe and wonder. Praising and thanking God just comes naturally.

So why do we have such a hard time praising and thanking God for who we are?

It's true, isn't it? So many of us have a skewed self-perception. Instead of feeling wonder, we wonder, *What's wrong with me?* Instead of feeling full of awe, we feel awful. Instead of feeling especially made, we convince ourselves, *I'm so boring.*

Some people have gone to the other extreme. You know the ones. They want praise for their looks, achievements, and talents—as though God had nothing to do with any of that. They're so full of themselves, there's no room for God.

Whether we are full of doubt or full of pride, it's as if we are looking in a warped mirror. We miss seeing what is really good, true, and beautiful about ourselves, and that keeps us from knowing who we really are. It keeps us from feeling wonder and gratitude. It keeps us from God.

God wants us to see ourselves with his eyes—with love

and joy. To see ourselves as his amazing, beloved creation. To fully appreciate who we are—and *whose* we are.

Instead of taking the blame or credit because of some skewed self-perception, we can think of ourselves as a work of art in his gallery. A lyric in his song. And the better we get to know and be our true selves, the more we help ourselves and others come to know and admire the Artist.

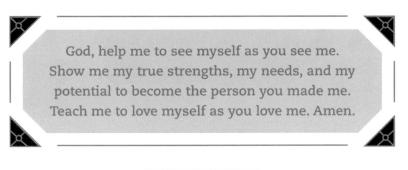

God, help me to see myself as you see me. Show me my true strengths, my needs, and my potential to become the person you made me. Teach me to love myself as you love me. Amen.

Digging Deeper

1. Jot down some thoughts about what you like most about yourself, your strengths, and your needs.
2. Is this perception of yourself realistic? Be honest. Do you think you might be too hard on yourself and miss seeing your many strengths? Or too full of yourself and miss seeing any of your weaknesses?
3. As you journal, ask the Holy Spirit for the wisdom and insight to know and love yourself as God planned.

God created the world to show forth and communicate his glory. That his creatures should share in his truth, goodness, and beauty—this is the glory for which God created them.

—CATECHISM OF THE CATHOLIC CHURCH, 319

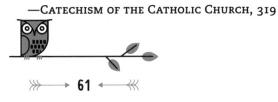

GOD IS TENDING ... I AM GROWING

27

For this is the will of God,
your sanctification.

—1 Thessalonians 4:3

What are your goals? Making the team? Getting married someday? We will have many short- and long-term goals, but our most important, lifelong goal is holiness.

Holiness? Isn't that for those saints with gold halos? Sure, but it's our goal too. God calls all of us to be saints.

Me? A saint? I don't have St. Francis of Assisi's compassion or St. Joan of Arc's courage.

Don't worry. God doesn't call us to be anyone but who we are and to be that well. A saint is simply someone who, with God's help, overcame their challenges, weaknesses, and circumstances and became who God made them to be, right where they were. It's like when gold is melted down to be refined. It's still gold, just *purer.* That's what holiness is. It's why artists painted golden halos as a sign of purity and holiness; it represented God's light and presence radiating from that person.

Holiness is what inspires us to admire these men and women of all ages, races, and walks of life. They weren't born saints. What made them so revered was a lifetime of work. Read their stories. Learn about their lives. These were ordinary people, just like you and me—who worked with God to develop extraordinary faith. Saints show us what is possible with God.

God knows that with his help, we can overcome our specific challenges, weaknesses, and circumstances. Even ones that seem impossible. Like Jesus says, "For God all things are possible."[1]

So set goals. Make short-term, long-term, and lifelong plans— but throughout them all, *strive for holiness.*

Be who you are and be that well.
—St. Frances de Sales

Ask God to refine you, to show you what to do right here and now, and he will help you become the saint he made you to be.

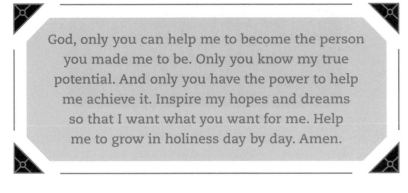

God, only you can help me to become the person you made me to be. Only you know my true potential. And only you have the power to help me achieve it. Inspire my hopes and dreams so that I want what you want for me. Help me to grow in holiness day by day. Amen.

Digging Deeper

By their examples, words, actions, convictions, and ongoing prayers, saints help us grow in faith.

1. What saint(s) do you feel close to, interested in, or at least curious about? Learn about their lives and love for God.
2. How did God work in and through them to help them to grow in holiness and become their best selves?
3. Choose a patron saint for this season of your life. Ask him or her to be your prayer partner—a holy helper, a mentor, and faithful friend for the journey.

---

1. Matthew 19:26

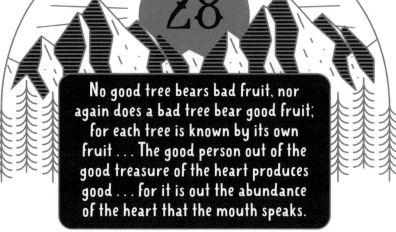

28

No good tree bears bad fruit, nor again does a bad tree bear good fruit; for each tree is known by its own fruit . . . The good person out of the good treasure of the heart produces good . . . for it is out the abundance of the heart that the mouth speaks.

—LUKE 6:43–45

Jesus isn't talking apples in these verses; he's talking about us. Whatever we hold in our hearts spills out in our actions and words. A bitter person rants and complains. Nothing is ever right or good enough. A person whose heart is full of anger has no peace or patience. Their words are abrupt, harsh, and harmful. And someone full of anxiety spins their worries and what ifs in ways that make things worse. Hanging with someone bitter, angry, or anxious soon has us feeling the same way. Clearly, bad fruit doesn't do anyone any good.

But unlike a tree, we have some say in the fruit we produce and inspire in others. So why not grow something great? Proverbs 4:23 tells us, "Keep your heart with all vigilance, for from it flow the springs of life." Being vigilant means we ask: *What is my heart holding on to? Is ripe with hope or rank with hate? Does it give me peace and joy or anxiety and despair?*

Just paying attention and noticing how we feel about

something helps us to see how it affects us and others around us. It helps us discern what is helpful from what is harmful.

Part of growing in holiness means taking our hearts to God and asking for his help. Often, we don't realize the lies we believe. The outrage we fuel. The regret and blame that bury us in guilt. God wants to free us from all that. When we ask for God's help through prayer and the sacraments of Reconciliation and the Eucharist, he prunes away all that is rotten. He enriches the soil of our hearts and helps to grow more of what is healthy and good.

> God, help me to root out any bitterness in my heart. Free me from lies, from envy, from anger and regret. Help me to be more loving, more kind, and more at peace. I want to grow more of your good fruit. Amen.

Digging Deeper

1. Are you feeling peace, or stress? Would others say you're kind, or kind of selfish? Be honest—do you feel the joy?
2. If we aren't intentional about what we are growing, chances are it's not all good. Read about the fruits of the spirit in Galatians 5:22–23. What do you need more of? Talk to God about it. Ask the Holy Spirit to help you bear his good fruit.

A tree is known by its fruit; a man by his deeds. A good deed is never lost; he who sows courtesy reaps friendship, and he who plants kindness gathers love.
—St. Basil

GOD IS TENDING ... I AM GROWING

29

> Happy are those who do not follow the advice of the wicked, or take the path the sinners tread, or sit in the seat of scoffers; but their delight is in the law of the Lord, and on his law they meditate day and night. They are like trees planted by streams of water, which yield their fruit in its season, and their leaves do not wither. In all that they do, they prosper.

—PSALM 1:1–3

We can get sidetracked online and end up down a random rabbit hole. Conversations can be like that too, often sliding into a mess of rumors and gossip.

As juicy info pops up like clickbait, we want to know all the details. *It's no big deal*, we tell ourselves. *I'm not going to tell anyone*. Even though we usually do. *Besides, what difference does it make if I know?* Well, a lot, actually.

The next time we see the person talked about, all that gossip comes to mind. True or not, those comments change how we see that person. Nothing good comes of gossip. It spreads like a destructive computer virus, corrupting as it goes.

God doesn't want us spreading lies and rumors. Instead, he wants to fill us with all that is good, beautiful, and true. And that comes by rooting ourselves in God's Word.

Read it. Think about it deeply. Pray with it daily. God's Word helps us know what he wants for us and from us. Keeping it fresh in our minds reminds of what to do when we aren't sure of something—*and* God's Spirit also works *through* the Word to *empower* us to do it.

Get rooted in God's Word. Soak it up. Not only will it guide us, feed us, and strengthen us, it will change us, and our world, for the better.

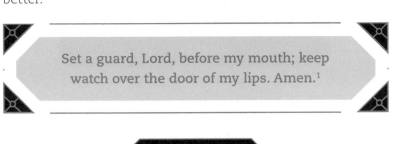

In that holy Writing you will find the Life of Jesus, but you should also find your own life there.

—St. Josemaría Escrivá

Set a guard, Lord, before my mouth; keep watch over the door of my lips. Amen.[1]

Digging Deeper

1. Here are some suggestions to help you get started reading God's Word:
   - read today's mass readings
   - read a whole gospel and focus on Jesus's life. (If you've never read one, start with the gospel of Mark.)
   - read one psalm a day (in five months, you'll have read all 150!)
2. Make a specific plan for reading Scripture. And if you miss a day, don't quit or stress out. As St. Benedict says, "Always, we begin again."

---

1. Paraphrase of Psalm 141:3

GOD IS TENDING ... I AM GROWING

30

> "'You shall love the Lord your God with all your heart, and with all your soul, and with all your mind.' This is the greatest and first commandment. And the second is like it: 'You shall love your neighbor as yourself.'"

—MATTHEW 22:37–39

In every class, it doesn't take long before someone asks the teacher, "Is this on the test?" We want to know what we *need* to know so that we get the answer *right*. But is getting all twenty multiple choice answers right the whole point? In a few weeks, we'll likely have forgotten most of what we'd memorized. (Ask your parents how many formulas they remember from a high school math class. Chances are, it's not many.) Memorizing right answers isn't as important as understanding big ideas. Because if we have figured out how to figure things out, we can find those answers whenever we need to.

Like school, life isn't about knowing all the right answers. It's about the ways we learn and grow from our experiences—and a lot of that happens through our mistakes. Our experiment failed. Our numbers didn't add up. But now we know to do it differently the next time.

It's the same with our faith. God wants us to know and do what is right. But that isn't enough. He tends to our hearts and minds to help us grow in understanding so that we do the right thing—for the right reason. For example, donating thirty cans for the food drive is doing the right thing. Donating them to impress your classmates is doing the right thing for the *wrong* reason. We were doing it out of love for ourselves, not love for others.

As God helps us to grow in our understanding of what is right and good, we see that it's not just about doing *what's right*, it's about *why* we do it. It's about *who* we are really doing it for.

Whenever you are feeling confused or unsure of what is right, remember God's big idea: love. Show love to others because of your love for God, and you won't go wrong.

God, forgive me for the times pride made me do right things for wrong reasons. Help me to focus less on myself and more on you so that I have right actions *and* right intentions. Let your love be my motivation. Amen.

Digging Deeper

Pride is a sneaky weed—we don't often notice it until it's taken over the garden of our hearts. So let's do a little uprooting and weeding out. Let's learn from our mistakes.

1. It's time to get real with a tough—and important—question: In the good that you do, are you seeking *God's glory* or *your own?*

It is not how much we do, but how much love we put in the doing. It is not how much we give, but how much love we put in the giving.

—St. Teresa of Calcutta

GOD IS TENDING ... I AM GROWING

R&R: Rest and Remember

Look back over what you read and wrote this week. What's your main takeaway?

_____

_____

_____

_____

_____

_____

_____

_____

_____

_____

WHO I AM

GOD IS ALL-KNOWING . . . I AM KNOWN

O LORD, you have searched me and known me.
You know when I sit down and when I rise up;
you discern my thoughts from far away. You
search out my path and my lying down, and are
acquainted with all my ways. Even before a word is
on my tongue, O LORD, you know it completely.
Amen.

—EXCERPT FROM PSALM 139

GOD IS ALL-KNOWING . . . I AM KNOWN

31

For the Lord does not see as mortals see; they look on the outward appearance, but the Lord looks on the heart.

—1 Samuel 16:7

It's always exciting when someone new joins class. We become curious, and we watch to see what they're like. If they crack jokes, we start to think they're funny. If they join the lunchtime football game, we assume they're athletic. How do they act? How are they dressed? Without even really trying to, we read their body language and get an overall gut feeling about them. *Shy. Confident. Nervous. Outgoing.*

Our first impressions are formed by what we observe. That's natural. It helps us connect with new people—people who are also forming first impressions about us. In a way, these first impressions are like rough drafts of friendships.

As we get to know each other better, these rough first impressions get edited and revised. We add new info. We tweak our assumptions. Yet no matter how many pieces we discover, we will never see the whole, complete picture like God does. We can read people's actions and try to fill in the gaps, but only God knows the whole story. Because God sees the heart. Not just our words and actions, but our thoughts and intentions.

So if we are ever feeling rejected, judged, or labeled by others, it's important to realize they don't know us. Not really. They are making assumptions based on what they've seen, heard, and pieced together so far. That's not who we truly are—it's who they *think* we are.

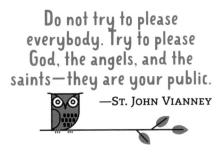

Do not try to please everybody. Try to please God, the angels, and the saints—they are your public.

—St. John Vianney

So pray about it. Ask God to show them the truth. Ask him to give you the courage to keep being true to yourself—and to give them the wisdom to see it.

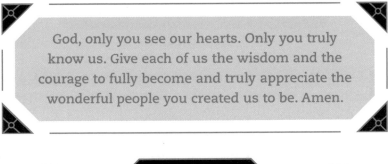

God, only you see our hearts. Only you truly know us. Give each of us the wisdom and the courage to fully become and truly appreciate the wonderful people you created us to be. Amen.

Digging Deeper

1. Do you feel rejected, judged, or labeled by others? Tell God about your hurt. Spend time with him and let him fill your heart with his healing love and acceptance.
2. Who might you be misjudging? Ask God to reveal what assumptions you might need to revisit and revise.

GOD IS ALL-KNOWING... I AM KNOWN

32

> O Lord, you have searched me and known me. You know when I sit down and when I rise up; you discern my thoughts from far away. You search out my path and my lying down, and are acquainted with all my ways.

—PSALM 139:1-3

Our best friends know us best. They know our likes and dislikes, our favorite movies, and our secret crushes—sometimes before we even tell them. A good friend can sense when we are feeling down or worried and they know the best way to cheer us up—simply because they understand us so well. We feel good around them because we feel seen, heard, and accepted just as we are (at least most of the time). A friendship like that is a safe place to be ourselves. But there is someone who knows us even more than our closest friends, even more than our families: God.

Who better to tune up an engine than the mechanic who built it? Who better to help us see the beauty and meaning in a work of art than the painter who created it? Who better to ask for help than someone who knows us, loves us, and ultimately wants us to be happy? If we want good advice, helpful feedback, or just the comfort of being seen, heard, and known—the best person we can turn to is always God.

God knows everything about us and he delights in all that we are. God knows us inside and out. Our past, our present, and our future. God knows our ways and our thoughts—the good and not so good. And he still loves us unconditionally. God even knows things we don't know about ourselves yet—our strengths, our talents and gifts, our passions and joys—and he so wants to help us discover them.

Part of being a teenager is figuring out who we truly are. We learn about ourselves through our closest relationships. We learn about our possible future

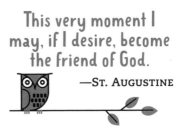

This very moment I may, if I desire, become the friend of God.

—St. Augustine

by trying new things, exploring new interests, and even discovering the things we don't do all that well. But the best way to learn about who we are, what we can do, why we are here, and how to live our best life is by asking God.

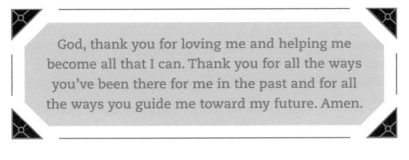

God, thank you for loving me and helping me become all that I can. Thank you for all the ways you've been there for me in the past and for all the ways you guide me toward my future. Amen.

Digging Deeper

1. Advice? Reassurance? Support? Someone who will listen? What do you most need right now?
2. Tell God all about it. Lean on him. Vent to him. Or just hang out with him and tell him how things are going.

GOD IS ALL-KNOWING ... I AM KNOWN

33

God, through Jesus Christ, will judge the secret thoughts of all.

—ROMANS 2:16

You better not pout, you better not cry, you better not shout, I'm telling you why . . .

As little kids, this song was a festive—and cautionary— reminder: Santa's coming, time to smarten up! So we did—or at least we tried to. No fighting with our brother—as much. No sulking—as long. We even might have done extra chores just to seal the deal. We didn't want a lump of coal. We had a whole wish list to earn!

We might see God in that same way. Not as a man in a red suit, but as the guy who is watching. Judging. Adding names to his naughty or nice list. Giving gifts to good kids and punishing bad ones. But if we only see God that way, we limit our understanding of him. We miss out on his mercy, love, and grace. Yes, God sees us and knows us. But unlike Santa, God doesn't want us to visit him once just to rhyme off our want list. He doesn't come one night a year, and only if we're sleeping. God isn't distant from us—and he doesn't want to be. He lives in us and wants to be a part of everything in our everyday lives. God wants a *real relationship* with us.

God does, however, bring gifts. An abundance of them,

beyond what we've asked. Because God knows exactly what we need and when we need it. His timing is always perfect.

We don't earn these gifts or even deserve them, really. God gives not because of what we do, but because of who he is: loving, generous, kind.

God wants us to be good—not to *get* something good, because he already knows we *are* something good. And with his help, we can truly know it and live it too.

God is more anxious to bestow His blessings on us than we are to receive them.

 —St. Augustine

---

God, I have been so blessed by you. Help me to recognize your goodness in my life. Help me to see your goodness in me and to live it out every moment of every day. Amen.

Digging Deeper

God knows exactly what you need. What blessings has he given you? Spend some time now thanking him for his goodness.

GOD IS ALL-KNOWING ... I AM KNOWN

34

> **Even before a word is on my tongue, O Lord, you know it completely.**
>
> —PSALM 139:4

If God already knows everything about us—what we think, how we feel, what we did, what we need—why pray? Good question. What is the point in telling anything to the One who knows everything?

We don't pray to inform God. But as we pray, God informs us. It's like talking with a friend or family member when we feel sad, frustrated, or confused. Talking about things with someone close doesn't just tell them what's in our hearts—it helps us discover it too. Sometimes the thing we thought was the problem isn't the problem at all. We may have felt angry about something—but as we talk, we realize though we've been acting angry, what we really feel is hurt or anxious. If we hadn't opened up and shared, we'd be stuck feeling angry for who knows how long. And we'd never deal with the real issue.

But God does more than just listen when we pray. If we turn to him and tell him what's on our hearts and minds—if we ask for his help—he works *in us* and in our lives. Things change. Hurts heal. Opportunities come. We find strength and courage. We get inspired. We feel hope or joy even in the middle of a struggle.

So pray. Often. Spend time with God each day. Talk, listen, or just be with him. It's how we get to know God better. It's how we get to know ourselves too.

You pay God a compliment by asking great things of Him.
—St. Teresa of Avila

God, when I am discouraged, hurt, or angry and reluctant to pray, help me remember you are there, you hear me, love me, and want to help me. Remind me to turn to you and lean on you, to open my heart and let you know how things are going. Amen.

Digging Deeper

We don't always want to talk about difficult things, but it helps. Especially when we take it to God. What is on your mind and heart today? Tell God about it. Give it to him and trust that he will take care of it because he cares for you.

GOD IS ALL-KNOWING ... I AM KNOWN

35

Before I formed you in the womb I knew you, before you were born I consecrated you; I appointed you a prophet to the nations.

—JEREMIAH 1:5

What do you want to be when you grow up?

Maybe you've always known; you wanted to be a firefighter as a little kid—and you still do now. Or maybe your newly discovered abilities and interests give you some direction. For example, you've noticed you are good with people and enjoy helping others, which makes you think you might enjoy being a teacher, social worker, or a nurse. For some of us, it's not that clear. We have a general goal in mind, but we don't know which specific career interests us. Or maybe, like a lot of people, you still have no idea. That unknown future can be scary and stressful if we're planners. A few more years of high school and then . . . *what's next?* Even the most confident graduate might second guess themselves: *What if I don't know what I want to do? What if I don't get into the program? What if it's too hard? What if . . . what if . . . what if . . .*

Thankfully, there's lots of time—lots of living to do—to help us figure out the road ahead. Maybe our job hasn't been invented yet. Who knows, we might even be the ones to invent it! We can drive ourselves crazy worrying about things that aren't in our control. The road ahead has too many twists and turns to see what lays around the bend. For all we know, our future holds a detour that takes us off-road on an unexpected adventure. One we can't plan for. But one we really enjoy.

The point is, God knows all we are and all we can become. He knows every wonderful thing waiting for us. He'll tell us where to go. And even if we take a wrong turn, God's Powerful Spirit—our GPS—is right there with us, recalculating for us, helping get us back on track.

With God as our guide, no matter where we are in life, we're never lost.

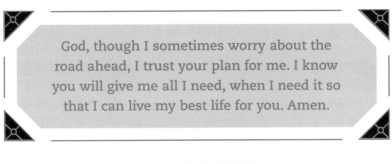

God, though I sometimes worry about the road ahead, I trust your plan for me. I know you will give me all I need, when I need it so that I can live my best life for you. Amen.

Digging Deeper

1. What are your hopes for the future?
2. What are your strengths and interests? What kind of work might be a good fit for those?
3. How does knowing God has a plan for you help to lessen your worries about the future?

Cast yourself into the arms of God and be very sure that if He wants anything of you, He will fit you for the work and give you strength.

—St. Philip Neri

GOD IS ALL-KNOWING ... I AM KNOWN

36

> You have kept a count of my tossings; put my tears in your bottle. Are they not in your record?
>
> —PSALM 56:8

When was the last time you cried? Did anyone comfort you? Did it feel like anyone cared?

Sometimes when we are dealing with something difficult, people try to help in ways that aren't helpful at all. We tell them what's going on and—instead of showing compassion, instead of really trying to help us out—they make it about them: *"You think that's bad? I had to . . . blah-blah-blah."*

Maybe they had good intentions or really wanted to help. But often, in trying to relate, people can take over the focus and our problem ends up ignored. That kind of help can leave us feeling worse. Because now, not only are we suffering through something, we think no one even cares.

But God cares. A lot.

Life is full of ups and downs. Beginnings and endings. Love and loss. Following God doesn't mean we won't have sad times or difficulties. But it does mean we aren't alone in them. God is always with us. Like David says, "This I know, that God is for me."[1] David also writes that God collects our tears and takes note of our struggles. Of course, God doesn't literally have a

---

1. Psalm 56:9

tear-filled jam jar with your name on it. But saying God collects our tears is a neat way of saying that God cares; our pain, our suffering, every one of our tears matters to him.

Conversations often help us to figure things out. But even when our friends can't "fix" the problem, it helps to feel heard. It's good to know someone is with us. That's why it's important to share how we feel with someone we trust.

But be sure to tell God too. Because only God fully sees and knows how you really feel. He knows the best way forward. And only God truly heals our deepest hurts.

> God, you know every tear I've ever cried, every hurt in my heart, and every hope I carry. In my lowest moments, help me to remember that I am not alone. You are with me, always. Heal me and give me your strength. Amen.

Digging Deeper

Sometimes, the words or actions of others can make us feel like we don't matter. But that doesn't make it true.

1. When was the last time you cried? What caused that pain?
2. How would it change things if you remembered God's truth? *God loves me. He's with me. I matter to him and with his help I can get through anything.*

Let us throw ourselves into the ocean of His goodness, where every failing will be canceled and anxiety turned into love.

—St. Paul of the Cross

GOD IS ALL-KNOWING . . . I AM KNOWN

R&R: Rest and Remember

Look back over what you read and wrote this week. What's your main takeaway?

_____

_____

_____

_____

_____

_____

_____

_____

_____

_____

WHY I AM SAFE

GOD IS TRUSTWORTHY ... I AM CONFIDENT

That your plan is better than anything else
Jesus, I trust in you.
That you always hear me and in your goodness always respond to me
Jesus, I trust in you.
That you give me the grace to accept forgiveness and to forgive others
Jesus, I trust in you.
That you give me all the strength I need for what is asked
Jesus, I trust in you.

—FROM THE SISTERS OF LIFE'S "LITANY OF TRUST"

GOD IS TRUSTWORTHY ... I AM CONFIDENT

37

To you, O Lord, I lift up my soul.
O my God, in you I trust.

—PSALM 25:1–2

Ever tried a trust fall? It's when we fold our arms, close our eyes, and fall back into the arms of the partner we *hope* will catch us. It shows that trusting means letting go of control and entrusting ourselves to another's help. We have confidence they will keep their promise to catch us and have the strength to do it. I mean, we're not going to fall into the arms of our five-year-old brother no matter how much we trust him, right?

If our partner fails and *literally* lets us down, we are much more cautious and reluctant to do it again. We learn from experience. And bruises. It's the same with relationships. Trusting someone with a secret, trusting someone with our heart—it all involves risk. We rely on their strength of character, on their abilities to be loyal and true. But even those closest to us can let us down at times. Maybe they lied. Maybe they weren't there for us like they promised. Maybe they put themselves first. In ways big and small, others can betray our trust, making it harder to trust them again.

Trust is built and rebuilt slowly over time. As we get to know the strength, character, and reliability of someone—we learn to trust them. Or not. But the person we can always trust to be present, to be faithful to his word and to us, is God.

God is trustworthy because of who he is. God is good. God is love. God doesn't lie, doesn't change, and *always* keeps his promises. When we read the Bible, we see time and again, generation after generation: how God was faithful to his people, how he loved them, and how he loves us.

We can abandon ourselves to God with total confidence. God's got our back and he will never let us down.

> God, thank you for having my back. I often forget your presence, strength, and wisdom and try to do everything myself. Teach me to rely on you, to lean on you, and to trust in you. Amen.

Digging Deeper

1. Who has broken your trust? Pray for that relationship. Ask God for his healing and guidance.
2. What's one small thing you can do to start rebuilding?
3. What are you trying to control in your life? Whatever the struggle, give it to God. Trust him with it and entrust yourself to his care.

Entrust yourself entirely to God. He is a Father and most loving Father at that, who would rather let heaven and earth collapse than abandon anyone who trusted in him.

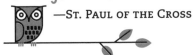 —St. Paul of the Cross

GOD IS TRUSTWORTHY ... I AM CONFIDENT

38

Jesus Christ is the same yesterday and today and for ever.

—HEBREWS 13:8

Ever see your grade 1 BFF years later and wonder what you had in common? You used to be inseparable, and now you hardly know each other. What happened? There was no drama or argument; you just drifted apart. You pursued different interests. Different friends. Different paths. And over time, you became different people. Some friendships are like that; here for a specific season of our lives.

But there is one relationship that is not seasonal. It's not limited to a specific age or time of our lives. And no matter how we grow and change, this relationship grows with us; enduring our whole life long. It's our relationship with Jesus.

Relationship? That might not be exactly how we'd describe it. Sure, we believe. We pray sometimes. We go to church now and then. We know *about* Jesus. But we don't feel we really *know him.*

None of that changes how Jesus feels about us. He is all in. Whether we are mildly curious or madly in love with him, Jesus is always there for us. He is a loyal and faithful friend. Always reaching out to us. Always longing to talk with us no matter how long it's been; it's never awkward with him. Wherever we are—he meets us there. He's the kind of friend who is excited to see us no matter how long we can stay. The kind that asks, *What's new? How's it going? You doing okay?*—and *really* wants to know.

No matter how much we change, or drift, or forget—Jesus is constant. His love. His presence. His support. His friendship. He freely gives it to each one of us. And as we accept, as we seek to know him more and more, Jesus helps us change for the better.

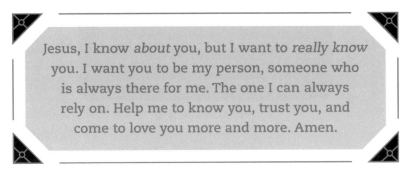

Jesus, I know *about* you, but I want to *really know* you. I want you to be my person, someone who is always there for me. The one I can always rely on. Help me to know you, trust you, and come to love you more and more. Amen.

Digging Deeper

1. What gospel story about Jesus is your favorite? Is it a miracle? A healing? A parable or teaching? Reread it now and think about what it reveals about Jesus. (For example, it might show that Jesus is powerful, loving, forgiving, inclusive, generous, or compassionate.)
2. How does that particular revelation about Jesus apply to your life right now?

He belongs to you, but more than that, he longs to be in you . . . He wants his breath to be in your breath, his heart in our heart, and his soul in your soul.

—St. John Eudes

GOD IS TRUSTWORTHY ... I AM CONFIDENT

39

Give thanks to him, bless his name.
For the Lord is good; his steadfast
love endures forever, and his
faithfulness to all generations.

—Psalm 100:4–5

We turn on the taps and expect hot water. We open the drawers, knowing they'll be clothes to wear. We know they'll be food in the cupboard even if we complain there's "nothing good to eat." The truth is: we've come to expect things to be the way they always are—an expectation that can make us ungrateful.

And it's not just about things. We know Mom will help us out with our project if we bring it to her—because she *always* does. We know Dad will make dinner for us—because he *always* cooks. We know our friend will come with us just because we asked—because they *always* do. In the same way, we can take their helpfulness, efforts, generosity—even their very presence—for granted.

We even do it with God. How easily we forget or take for granted God's blessings in our lives, like our homes and belongings, our food, family, and friends—even life itself. When we do, we miss out. We don't appreciate, we just consume. We ignore and forget. Most of all, we complain when things aren't the way we expect. *Where's God?* we whine, as though God was the one who left us. In the end, we feel doubt and distrust. And we do it all without even thinking. Actually, we do it *because* we aren't thinking.

When we are feeling discouraged, doubtful, and reluctant to trust God, it's a sign we've forgotten who God is. We've forgotten what God has done—and is still doing—for us.

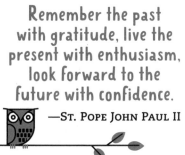

Remember the past with gratitude, live the present with enthusiasm, look forward to the future with confidence.

—St. Pope John Paul II

The antidote to those feelings of doubt and distrust is *awareness*. It's that simple. Make an effort to notice, remember, and appreciate the people and everyday blessings in your life. Just see them. And say *thanks!*

Because awareness leads to gratitude and gratitude leads to joy.

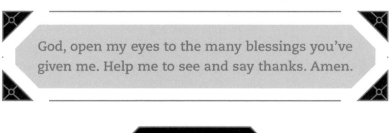

God, open my eyes to the many blessings you've given me. Help me to see and say thanks. Amen.

Want an attitude of gratitude? Want to feel more joy in your everyday life? Start keeping a daily gratitude list. Each day, simply add five new things—big or small—you're thankful for. Once you start looking, you'll be amazed at all the blessings you hadn't noticed before.

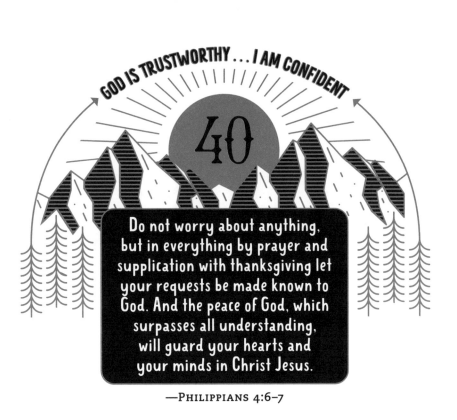

GOD IS TRUSTWORTHY ... I AM CONFIDENT

40

Do not worry about anything, but in everything by prayer and supplication with thanksgiving let your requests be made known to God. And the peace of God, which surpasses all understanding, will guard your hearts and your minds in Christ Jesus.

—PHILIPPIANS 4:6–7

We've learned through experience that flicking that switch brings light. Like most people, we can't explain exactly *how* electrical power surges through the wires and illuminates the bulb, but that doesn't make us any less confident in it. When things get dark, we don't freak out . . . or worry . . . or doubt. We simply reach out and turn on the light. It's that simple.

So why don't we approach God with the same confidence?

For some reason, we'd rather wallow in our worries than ask for God's guidance. We let ourselves be overshadowed by anxiety and stress instead of choosing to rest in God's peace. It's like we get ourselves so stressed out, so worked up, so burnt out from being so focused on the dark—that we entirely forget about the light. We forget that God is there.

And God is there. Right with us. He can and will help us. In fact, he longs to. God is just waiting to empower us, enlighten us, and fill us with his peace. But first, we have to remember to ask for it.

Try it and see. Because what have we got to lose, really? Worry? Anxiety? Stress? Sounds good to me.

Not only will God answer with his power and presence, the amazing thing is the more we turn to God, the more confident our prayers become. We will know from experience that prayer works. That God hears. That God answers. Because we know God loves.

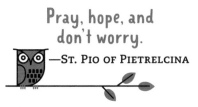

Pray, hope, and don't worry.

—St. Pio of Pietrelcina

So why stay in dark with all those fears and worries? Plug in to God's endless power supply, be enlightened, and shine!

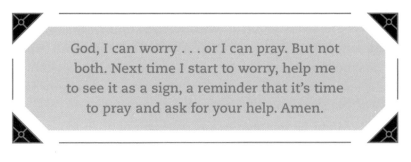

God, I can worry . . . or I can pray. But not both. Next time I start to worry, help me to see it as a sign, a reminder that it's time to pray and ask for your help. Amen.

Digging Deeper

1. What worry is on your mind these days?
2. Turn on the light—take it to God and ask for his help.

41

> May the God of hope fill you with all joy and peace in believing, so that you may abound in hope by the power of the Holy Spirit.
>
> —ROMANS 15:13

Although God always hears and answers our prayers, if it's not in the way or the timing we expect, we might grow anxious and even doubtful. We prayed to make the volleyball team but got cut. We prayed to pass a math test but still failed. Or maybe we prayed for our aunt to get better but her cancer continues to spread. In times like these, we can wonder where God is. *Did God hear? Will he help? Does God even care?*

We might be tempted to feel let down or abandoned. And if we continue to think and feel this way, we'll start trusting God less and less. That is exactly what the devil wants. This enemy wants us to feel anxious, alone, and abandoned by God. But that doesn't mean it's true. Far from it.

In those challenging times, we need to trust God even more. Trust God is with us even if we can't feel it. Trust God is at work even if we can't see it. A trust like that, in hard times, sounds like some kind of superpower. And actually, it is. It's the Holy Spirit's superpower working in us and through us.

Like an engine boost in the harshest weather, the Holy Spirit works in our hearts and recharges our strength. He jolts our memories of all the ways God has been faithful in the past. In doing so, the Holy Spirit helps us trust God is still faithful and present, however things may seem. With the Holy Spirit's help we can believe wholeheartedly that everything is in God's hands. And like St. Paul says, "We know that all things work together for good for those who love God, who are called according to his purpose."[1]

> God, when I pray and don't see results right away, my impatience turns to doubt. In these low moments, strengthen me with your Spirit. Remind me of who you are and all you have done in my life. Renew my hope and confidence in you. Amen.

Digging Deeper

A great way to remember who God is and what he's done is by keeping a prayer journal. Jot down your daily prayers and intentions and include updates of when and how God answered. Because God *always* hears and *always* answers prayers in his time and wisdom. We can trust he knows best.

> You [God] are a Fire that takes away the coldness, illuminates the mind with its light, and causes me to know your truth.
> —St. Catherine of Sienna

---

1. Romans 8:28

GOD IS TRUSTWORTHY ... I AM CONFIDENT

42

Rekindle the gift of God that is within you ... for God did not give us a spirit of cowardice, but rather a spirit of power and of love and of self-discipline.

—2 TIMOTHY 1:6–7

As toddlers, we'd shove our broken toy in Mom or Dad's lap. "Fix it? Fix it. *FIX IT!*" We wanted everything to be okay again—and we wanted it *now!* In some ways, not much has changed. Instead of worrying about a broken toy, we worry about broken friendships and broken promises. We stress over fitting in or being left out. We are anxious about final assignments or final cuts. But mostly, we worry about what everyone thinks about us: *Am I popular enough? Am I smart enough?* Or simply: *Am I enough?* We worry about living up to expectations. About what happened in the past, what's going on now, and what will happen in the future. We have a lot going on.

But the real question is: what do we do with these concerns? Do we take them to God—or do we let our minds spin and make things worse? And when we take our fears and anxieties to God and lay them in his in lap, do we just . . . leave them there?

God will take care of things in his time and his way. But

we often want it right now, crying fix-it-*fix-it*-*FIX-IT!!* until we can't wait any more and snatch back the worry.

God knows what needs fixing. He knows how. He knows when. And he encourages us to wait on him. "Wait for the Lord; be strong, and let your heart take courage; wait for the Lord!"[1]

As we mature, we learn not to let our feelings control us. We realize we have God's power and self-discipline within us. We may feel anxious—but we choose to trust God instead. We may feel impatient—but we choose to wait. With every good choice, we grow stronger, more patient, more peaceful. And with practice, trusting him the next time becomes even easier.

Patience is the companion of wisdom.
—St. Augustine

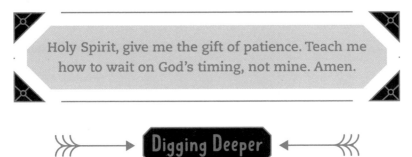

Holy Spirit, give me the gift of patience. Teach me how to wait on God's timing, not mine. Amen.

Digging Deeper

What are some ways you can start using God's powerful gifts of love and self-discipline in your everyday life?

---

1. Psalm 27:14

GOD IS TRUSTWORTHY . . . I AM CONFIDENT

R&R: Rest and Remember

Look back over what you read and wrote this week. What's your main takeaway?

_____

_____

_____

_____

_____

_____

_____

_____

_____

_____

_____

WHY I AM SAFE

GOD IS EVER-PRESENT . . . I AM SAFE

Lord, I worship you as my first beginning, I long for you as my last end, I praise you as my constant helper, and call on you as my loving protector. Guide me by your wisdom, correct me with your justice, comfort me with your mercy, protect me with your power.

— FROM THE UNIVERSAL PRAYER
OF POPE CLEMENT XI

GOD IS EVER-PRESENT . . . I AM SAFE

43

You hem me in, behind and before,
and lay your hand upon me.

—PSALM 139:5

Remember getting lost when you were a kid? You're out shopping with Mom or Dad, you get distracted for just a second, and the next thing you know . . . they're *gone!* What a terrifying realization. You called their names. You ran aisle to aisle. You scanned the crowds for their familiar faces—but everyone around you was a stranger.

Who's going to help me? Your little heart and mind raced. *Where do I go? What do I do?*

Being lost, afraid, and confused makes us also feel totally alone. And it doesn't only happen when we are small. We don't get lost in the store anymore (hopefully) but we can still feel lost, afraid, and completely alone when we face important decisions and choices.

Should I speak up or keep it secret? Do I go or not? Do I say yes or no? What's right? What's the best choice? What should I do next?

The more we worry about making the wrong choice, the worse those feelings get. But no matter how lost and confused we might feel about our struggles, it helps to remember we aren't alone. Actually, we aren't even lost because God is there with us. He is hemmed around us. He encircles us.

Think about that for a second: we are safe in God's forcefield of love. God's got our back—and what's more, God's got a plan. That means that no matter how far off track we've wandered or how many wrong turns we've made, God can and will help us find our way forward. He will make everything work out for our good if we just ask for his help.

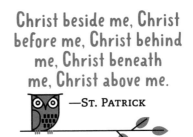

Christ beside me, Christ before me, Christ behind me, Christ beneath me, Christ above me.

—St. Patrick

God, when I get overwhelmed with worry and fear, remind me you are there with me. Help me remember that I am safe, encircled in your love. Give me your wisdom to decide which way to go and the courage to take it. Amen.

1. What is making you feel confused, lost, or afraid lately?
2. How would it change things to know that God is with you and for you? Talk to God about it and ask for his help.

44

> The Lord is my rock, my fortress, and my deliverer, my God, my rock in whom I take refuge, my shield, and the horn of my salvation, my stronghold.

—PSALM 18:1–2

The psalm writers chose images from their daily lives to represent God's strength and protection: God is a rock. A fortress and stronghold. A shield. A shepherd standing watch against the wolves. A mother bird's wings. If we wrote our own psalm about God's presence and protection, we might choose a symbol we know better, like a superhero. Superheroes don't stand by—they step up. They defend those in need. They protect all that is good. What a great symbol for God, our personal, all-powerful champion against every evil.

Our superhero, God, even has superpowers. He's all-seeing and all-knowing. He can read minds and hearts. He knows our future and our past. God is also all-powerful; no kryptonite will ever weaken him. God doesn't use a mask to protect his identity because he *wants* to be recognized and known by us. And God wants to be our champion against everything—whatever disturbs our calm, whatever steals our joy, and whatever chokes our hope—both outside and within us. The lies. The gossip. The mocking. All those mean attacks that come when we least expect it. The hatred, doubts, and despair the enemy uses against us. God wants to bring us into the safety of his forcefield of love and peace where none of those things touch our hearts. The closer we get to God, the less those villainous words matter because we can clearly hear his loving words the loudest.

So trust God to be your hero. He has already saved you from sin and death. Send out the "bat-signal." Call on his name. God is always ready and willing at any moment to protect, defend, and guard you against every evil.

> **God is a spring of living water which flows unceasingly into the hearts of those who pray.**
>
> —ST. LOUIS GRIGNION DE MONTFORT

Holy Spirit, inspire my imagination with a deeper understanding of all God is and all God does for me. Amen.

Digging Deeper

1. God protects, guides, and raises us up. He provides, heals, and restores. What are some action words to describe what God has done for you lately?

2. What everyday symbols might represent those action words? For example, a helmet protects, a GPS guides, a trampoline raises us up higher than we can go ourselves. Choose one symbol and write your own psalm prayer. *The Lord is my . . .*

GOD IS EVER-PRESENT... I AM SAFE

45

Why are you afraid, you of little faith?

—MATTHEW 8:26

few of the disciples were experienced fishermen. They knew how to sail in any weather. But a particular storm overwhelmed them. It came out of nowhere: Dark clouds. Whipping winds. Enormous waves. The men panicked as the water crashed over the sides and started filling the bottom of the boat, afraid they were going to sink.

"Lord, save us!" they cried, waking Jesus for help. Jesus asked them why they're afraid; didn't they know they were safe with him? Then, at his word, the storm ended and all was calm.

At times in our lives, like the disciples we can feel overwhelmed and afraid by our circumstances. It could be getting unexpected bad news. The loss of a loved one. A situation where we feel powerless and full of fear. Our storm might even be made up of all those stresses of everyday life that suddenly feel too much to cope with: homework, deadlines, work schedules, friend drama, chores, and house rules that seem so unfair. In those moments, our anxiety and fear threaten to overwhelm us.

But like all Gospel scenes, the storm is there to show us who Jesus is. Who God is. Because what Jesus does for those disciples, he can do for us. The more we read the Gospels, the better we understand that connection. Jesus knows how it feels to grieve, to be ridiculed and rejected, to be misunderstood and betrayed. He's lived through it all, and he is with us, ready to help us through our storms too. Whatever the storm, we can confidently turn to Jesus for help knowing he will give it.

The Prince of Peace is always in our boat, in our life, and in our heart. He is in that storm with us, waiting for us to call on him. All we have to do is say those three words: "Lord, save me!"

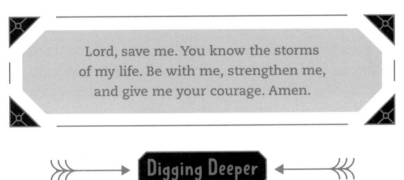

Lord, save me. You know the storms of my life. Be with me, strengthen me, and give me your courage. Amen.

Digging Deeper

1. What is your current storm? How does it make you feel?
2. Now, picture Jesus standing by you in it. Know that you are not alone. See Jesus taking control in whatever storm you're in—those within and without. Hear Jesus speak his peace to calm your heart. What is he telling you?

We shall steer safely through every storm, as long as our heart is right, our intention fervent, our courage steadfast, and our trust fixed in God.
—St. Francis de Sales

GOD IS EVER-PRESENT . . . I AM SAFE

46

"Take heart, it is I; do not be afraid."

—MATTHEW 14:27

Windswept waves battered the ship's hull as the disciples crossed the sea. This time they were sailing without Jesus. Suddenly, Peter saw something— no, some*one*—walking on the water. All the men were terrified.

"Take heart," Jesus said as he approached them, "it is I; do not be afraid."

Could it be? Peter wasn't sure, so he called across the water, saying that if you really are Jesus, tell me to come to you. So Jesus called to him. And Peter climbed out of his comfort zone, out of the boat into the unknown. Peter's heart must have been pounding as he took that first step. Yet, somehow, he did. Eyes on Jesus, Peter took another step. And another.

But as the wind gusted around Peter's trembling legs, as the cold waves splashed over his feet, as he considered how dark and deep the sea was beneath him—Peter's fears took over. *This is crazy!* he must have thought. *What am I doing? I can't do this! I'm going to sink!*

He let his doubts speak louder than the truth. His fears about what *might* happen took his attention away from the what *actually was* happening; Peter was walking on water, thanks to Jesus. But instead of seeing and believing in what

Jesus could do through him, Peter's focused on what he himself could not do. And that's when he started to sink.

In the same way, when we focus on our fears and doubts, they overwhelm us. Our hearts sink. We can drown in those what-ifs or we can keep our eyes on Jesus. Jesus calls us beyond our comfort zones in many ways: To speak up. To reach out. To take that first step knowing he will give us the strength to keep going. All we need to do is get out of the boat and keep our eyes on him. Call on him, knowing he is there, ready to help. Knowing that through him, we can do this step by step.

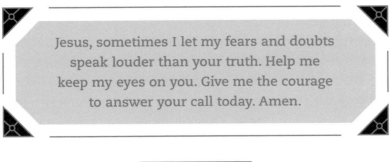

Do not be afraid! Life with Christ is a wonderful adventure.
—St. Pope John Paul II

Jesus, sometimes I let my fears and doubts speak louder than your truth. Help me keep my eyes on you. Give me the courage to answer your call today. Amen.

Digging Deeper

1. Write about your comfort zone. What next step is Jesus asking of you?
2. What does he want you to trust him with?

GOD IS EVER-PRESENT... I AM SAFE

47

Do not fear, only believe.

—MARK 5:36

We might think that a courageous person never feels afraid. That being brave or fearless comes naturally to them and not to us. But that's not true.

Courage is not the *absence* of fear. Courage is the *choice* to keep going, to keep moving forward *despite* our feelings. It means recognizing we might be anxious or afraid—but not wallowing in it or being paralyzed by it. Courage means choosing to push past worries that make us doubt ourselves and second-guess our God-given abilities. It means remembering that if God is calling us to experience or endure something, he will also give us what we need to make it through. Courage means acknowledging our concerns and fears, bringing them to God, and finding the strength in him to do what needs doing. Every time we choose to rely on God and not our insecurities, we grow stronger and more courageous because we remember how God helped us through challenges the last time.

Maybe that's why God tells us not to fear over a hundred times in the Bible. God says it to Abraham, Hagar, and Isaac.[1] To Moses and Joshua.[2] To Isaiah and Jeremiah.[3] To Mary, Joseph,

---

1. Genesis 15:1; 21:17; 46:3
2. Number 21:34; Joshua1:9
3. Isaiah 41:10; Jeremiah 1:8

and the shepherds.[4] And Jesus says it many, many times to his disciples and to us: "Do not fear, only believe."[5] This is why these people had the courage to do amazing things—to trust when things seemed hopeless. To persevere when things seemed pointless. To have great courage in the face of great uncertainty—all because they chose faith over fear. They chose to believe God's promise.

As we read God's Word, we meet these people. We learn their stories and circumstances. We are inspired by how God worked in their lives. And we are en-*couraged* to say yes to all the ways God wants to work in our lives too.

> God, when I am afraid, help me to focus less on what *I can't* do and more on what *you can* do. Help me to push through my insecurities knowing you are with me and you give me whatever I need to do your will right here and now. Amen.

 Digging Deeper

1. What is one area where you need help choosing faith over fear?
2. Talk to God about it. Ask him for his strength.

Therefore with mind entire, faith firm, courage undaunted, love thorough, let us be ready for whatever God wills.

 —St. Bede the Venerable

---

4. Luke 1:30; Matthew 1:20; Luke 2:9-10
5. Mark 5:36

GOD IS EVER-PRESENT . . . I AM SAFE

48

Therefore I tell you, do not worry about your life.

—MATTHEW 6:25

Worry often seems to be our default setting. Mainly we worry about what others think of us, which social media makes even worse. When we post something, we keep compulsively checking to see how people respond. *Did they see it? Do they like it? Did they share it?* We want to fit in, be accepted, and appreciated, and we worry we won't be good enough, popular enough, or smart enough.

Other times we worry we can't cope with whatever is going on in our lives. It might be family drama, illness, or a difficult change. Whatever the worries, they are all rooted in that feeling of powerlessness. We want to control everything in our lives—but the truth is we can't.

So what do we do about it? We worry.

Worry means we are trying to figure out and fix things that are often beyond our control. But *all* worry is *useless*. Think about it; nothing has ever improved because we worried about it. The only outcome of worry is feeling worse.

Jesus tells us not to worry and to trust in faith that God knows and provides exactly what we need, and will answer how and when we need it. When we pray instead of worrying, we give our concerns to God. We let go of that urge to control.

We rest, knowing our particular problem is in the hands of the all-powerful One who can and will help because he loves us.

We can worry. Or we can pray. But we can't do both. So if you want to worry less—pray more.

God, I worry about a lot of things. Teach me how to shift from worry to prayer. When I start to feel stressed, nudge my heart and remind me to give it all to you. Amen.

Digging Deeper

Get in the habit of telling God about your worries right away as part of your daily prayer, before they become a burden of worry and stress.

1. What's on your mind today? What are you feeling anxious or stressed about? Tell God about it. Leave it with him knowing he'll take care of it. And you.

It is our part to seek, his to grant what we ask; ours to make a beginning, his to bring it to completion; ours to offer what we can; his to finish what we cannot.

—St. Jerome

GOD IS EVER-PRESENT ... I AM SAFE

R&R: Rest and Remember

Look back over what you read and wrote this week. What's your main takeaway?

_____

_____

_____

_____

_____

_____

_____

_____

_____

_____

WHY I AM SAFE

GOD IS MERCIFUL ... I AM FORGIVEN

Heavenly King, Consoler Spirit, Spirit of Truth, present everywhere and filling all things, treasure of all good and source of all life, come dwell in us, cleanse us and save us, you who are All-Good.

—Catechism of the Catholic Church

GOD IS MERCIFUL... I AM FORGIVEN

49

You shall put these words of mine in your heart and soul.

—DEUTERONOMY 11:18

Imagine a soccer game where the rules kept changing. As you're kicking the ball up the field, your opponent grabs the ball, tucks in under his arm like a football, and takes off running. Next time you get the ball, another player knocks you flat on your back with a roundhouse kick but no foul is called. Then, right as you're about to score, the goalie and his buddies take off with the net. Not much of a game, is it? Rules exist for a reason, even in soccer. Knowing the boundaries, the expectations, and the consequences of breaking them helps players respect the game and each other. This kind of fair play also allows each player to develop their skills and have fun doing it. It's what makes soccer *soccer*.

In the same way, we have rules for life: the Ten Commandments.[1] Now, we might think these ancient tablets given to Moses thousands of years ago don't really apply to us. Besides, it's not like we're murderers, adulterers, and thieves, right? But let's dig a little deeper. Because these boundaries and expectations, and the consequences of breaking them, are God's guidelines for a great life. Following the

---

1. Exodus 20:2-17; Deuteronomy 5:6-21

commandments—taking God's coaching—is how we develop character, connection, and find real joy.

Each commandment is more than a simple do or don't. Think about what each command protects and upholds. For instance, we may not be thieves, but have we cheated on a test or illegally downloaded movies or songs? We may not kill, covet, or give false witness—but are we judgmental, jealous, and eager to gossip? Are we genuinely happy when good things happen to others? Do we respect our parents' rules? Most importantly, do we let other things or people take the place of God in our lives?

Do you know that often a root has split a rock when allowed to remain in it? Give no place to the seed of evil, seeing that it will break up your faith.

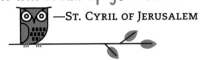

—St. Cyril of Jerusalem

If we spend time thinking about each of God's Commandments, we see the gift of this rulebook. One that teaches us how respect the game of life, the Giver of Life, and every player in the league.

> God, thank you for all the ways you coach me in holiness. Thanks also for the many times you forgive me when I fall short. Give me the desire and the strength to keep trying to live by your will. Amen.

Digging Deeper

Reread the Ten Commandments (Exodus 20:2-17). As you read, think about how they help to guide you in your life.

GOD IS MERCIFUL...I AM FORGIVEN

50

But you, O Lord, are a God merciful and gracious, slow to anger and abounding in steadfast love and faithfulness.

—PSALM 86:15

We said something hurtful. *But it was funny.* We included everyone but her. *But she's just so annoying.* We didn't tell our parents the whole story. *But, technically, it isn't lying.* Our brains try to rationalize it, but our hearts know better.

If we eat something off, our stomach lets us know. It urges us to *get it out!* Our hearts—or conscience—works in a similar way. Sin is rotten. It makes us sick. The more we sin and try to ignore it, the more it seems to poison our thoughts. That helpful sense of guilt or regret we feel at first, if ignored, will fester into shame and blame. Then, instead of just noticing what we did wrong, we start defining ourselves by it:

I'm such a loser. No wonder no one likes me.
I'll never do anything right. I'm just no good.
God will never forgive me for this.

All lies, of course. But for some reason, our self-pity makes us believe them. At times, we might even think we don't deserve to be forgiven—and, honestly, we don't. None of us deserve it. But thankfully, God's forgiveness isn't based on our worthiness, it's based on his mercy—and that is an endless supply.

Mercy is compassion and kindness. But it's more than a feeling of love; it's the willingness to help anyone in need. In this case, our need is forgiveness and healing—and God longs to meet it. God wants to forgive us and heal us. He wants to give us his grace and power to do better and grow stronger. But first, we have to ask.

Our sins are nothing but a grain of sand alongside the great mountain of the mercy of God.

—ST. JOHN VIANNEY

It's time we examine what rotten sins might be on our conscience and then take them to God. Go to confession, take all that rotten garbage out. Then we can be filled even more with God's goodness.

> God, please give me the courage to apologize and confess. Inspire my words and actions so I can make things right. Thanks for loving me no matter what and for always giving me another chance. With your help, I know I can do better. Amen.

Digging Deeper

1. How might your words or actions have hurt someone this week?
2. How might these things be hurting you?
3. What will you do to make things right?

GOD IS MERCIFUL... I AM FORGIVEN

51

> "Let us eat and celebrate; for this son of mine was dead and is alive again; he was lost and is found!" And they began to celebrate.

—LUKE 15:23–24

Every sin leaves its mark. A smudge of selfishness. A smear of pride. Hardly noticeable as we go about our day. But these sins accumulate like grime on a window. It isn't until we really look that we realize how dirty that window has gotten. Look how it's dimmed the light. Notice how it limits our view?

An examination of conscience helps us to see the dirt of sin on our souls. We ask for the Holy Spirit's help to remind us of the ways we might have let God and others down. As we pray, we remember specific times we sinned.

Maybe we were like the prodigal son from Jesus's parable. Did we take God for granted? Were we ungrateful? Were we so focused on what we wanted from God there was no room for God? How far or how long did we wander away?

Or maybe we were like the older brother. Yes, he stays and works for his father. But he's also full of pride and self-righteousness. Instead of joining the party, the older brother sulks outside. He won't join because he's jealous and judgmental toward his wayward brother, thinking he's better than him. Because of these sins, the older brother misses seeing and celebrating the good.

Before God can forgive us, we need to see what needs cleaning in our hearts, minds, and lives. We might not feel like doing an examination of conscience. I mean, who wants to be reminded of their sins? It is so much *easier* to ignore it all, right? But the point of washing a window is not to focus on the grime or dwell on how it got dirty. The goal is to make it clean.

And noticing the dirt is the first step.

> God, I know I've been avoiding the dirt of my sins. Send me your Spirit. Give me the insight to see how I have wronged you and others. Give me the courage to do my part in seeking forgiveness and in making things right. With your help, I know I can do better. Amen.

Digging Deeper

1. Read the parable of the prodigal son in Luke 15:11–32. Picture Jesus saying it to you. What part, what line, or even what word strikes you about this story today? What takeaway do you think Jesus wants you to have?
2. Do an examination of conscience. On page 211, you'll find a helpful guide.

> **Sooner or later we have to seek forgiveness. If the evil which we have done involves other people, we have to ask their forgiveness too; but for the guilt to be truly remitted, we always have to receive forgiveness from God.**
>
> —St. Pope John Paul II

GOD IS MERCIFUL... I AM FORGIVEN

52

> But if we walk in the light as he himself is in the light, we have fellowship with one another, and the blood of Jesus his Son cleanses us from all sin.

—1 John 1:7

God told Adam and Eve *not* to eat from that tree, but they did it anyway, knowing it was against God's wishes. That's a pretty clear example of sin: knowing God's will and choosing to go against it. But sin does more than "break the rules"—it breaks relationships. When Adam and Eve made their selfish choice, there were consequences. That choice and act affected their holiness. It cost them their perfect life in Eden. But worst of all, their sin separated them from God.

Every sin we commit separates us a bit more from God too. He still loves us and longs to be with us. But each time we go against what we know is right, loving, and true—against who God is—it's like taking another step away. Sin by sin, we move farther away from God and from who he made us to be.

At heart, we are not liars, even though we sometimes lie. We are not selfish, even though we often put ourselves first. We are not bad, even though we sometimes sin. But if we make enough of those mistakes, and leave them unchecked, we'll start to think that's who we really are. So remember the truth:

We are made in God's image. We are good. We are loving. That's who we are, even when our sinful actions go against our true selves.

Jesus came to lead us back home to God, who is eagerly waiting to celebrate our return. Because of Jesus, and all he did for us, we can be forgiven. That doesn't just mean our souls are wiped clean—it means we are healed of *everything* that comes with sin. No more guilt or shame. Thanks to Jesus's sacrifice and God's mercy, we are restored and we can begin again: With God. With one another. And with renewed hope.

> God, I know my sins have hurt you and others. And I know my guilt and shame has hurt me. Please forgive me. Help me to remember the truth about myself: *I am good. I am loving. I am yours.* And help me to live that truth choice by choice, day by day. Amen.

Digging Deeper

1. In what ways have your sins separated you from others?
2. How does your selfishness, your [pride, envy, lust, laziness, anger, gluttony, or greed] hurt your most important relationships? What will you do about it?

Sin severs the relationship with God and it severs the relationship with brothers and sisters, relationships within the family, in society and in the community: sin always severs; it separates; it divides.
—POPE FRANCIS

GOD IS MERCIFUL ... I AM FORGIVEN

53

Create in me a clean heart, O God, and put a new and right spirit within me.

—PSALM 51:10

Imagine being in the store that sells super expensive crystal. You know the stuff: Etched wine glasses. Delicate vases. Those crazy-priced sculptures. All of it dangerously perched on wobbly shelves. And there's you, lumbering about with your overstuffed backpack. You probably should have paid attention to the sign: *Leave bags outside.*

Next thing you know, your bag bumps a display and—CRASH!—the whole thing smashes to the ground. The store manager looks over and your stomach sinks. You know *someone* has to pay for this and there's no way you can. Even if you saved every paycheck, even if you took on extra work babysitting or cutting lawns, you'd never come close to making enough.

Then a guy comes into the store and says, "I got this." He hands the manager his credit card. And just like that, your debt is paid. Your mistake is amended. You're free.

Sometimes we feel like our mistakes can't be undone and we've ruined everything. In those lowest moments, we can sit and feel the sting of those sharp edges of guilt or shame. Shame scars us—but it doesn't change what happened. Only

Jesus can. Jesus walks into the middle of our mess and takes it from us. "I've got this," he says, paying for our mistakes. Just because he loves us. Because he wants to free us from the burden of it. Because he wants us to feel better and do better. Because he knows we *are* better.

Instead of trying to pretend nothing happened or sitting in our guilt or shame, Jesus invites us to take our sins to God and receive the sacrament of Reconciliation, knowing however big or little the damage, the debt has already been paid. Our conscience is cleared. Our hearts are healed and whole again. Thanks to Jesus.

And through him, God gives us his grace: the forgiveness, peace, and strength to know better and do better next time.

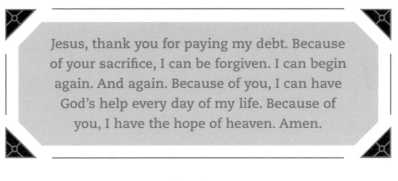

Jesus, thank you for paying my debt. Because of your sacrifice, I can be forgiven. I can begin again. And again. Because of you, I can have God's help every day of my life. Because of you, I have the hope of heaven. Amen.

Digging Deeper

What's your broken crystal? What mistakes are you holding on to and hurting yourself with even more? Jesus wants to help you let that go. Tell him. Trust him. He's got this.

In the Sacrament of Reconciliation Christ has given us a great gift. If we use it faithfully, it becomes an inexhaustible source of new life. Do not forget this!
—ST. POPE JOHN PAUL II

GOD IS MERCIFUL... I AM FORGIVEN

54

Bear with one another and, if anyone has a complaint against another, forgive each other; just as the Lord has forgiven you, so you also must forgive.

—COLOSSIANS 3:13

We know what it's like to be forgiven. To be freed from that weight of guilt. To know we've been given a second chance, a new start. It feels like a spring day after a long, dark winter. Hopefully, we experience it regularly. Because any time and every time we examine our conscience and go to Reconciliation with a desire to do better, God forgives us.

But Jesus doesn't just call us to be forgiven, he calls us to *forgive*. And sometimes that is even harder. How do we let go of deep hurt caused by someone close? How do we forget that painful social media post or the fact our so-called friends posted and reposted it? How do we get over our resentment at being so betrayed, abandoned, or ignored?

There's no denying—it all hurts. Deeply. Like any wound, a broken relationship takes time to heal. Lots of time. But in the meantime, we can still forgive.

Wait . . . what?! Are you kidding me?! Forgive them? Do you know what they did, what they said, how they hurt me? Maybe they don't deserve forgiveness. Maybe they aren't even asking for it.

Sometimes people don't even realize what they've done wrong. But none of that stops us from forgiving them—because forgiveness isn't a feeling, it's a *choice*.

Even as he hung on the cross, Jesus forgave the soldiers who'd nailed him there. Even as they gambled to see who got his clothes, even as they nailed up a sign to mock him, even as they watched him die and never felt a moment of regret—Jesus forgave them completely.

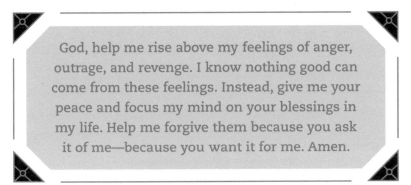

To withhold forgiveness is to take poison and expect the unforgiven to die.

—St. Augustine

Like Jesus, we are called to choose forgiveness. It might be difficult. It will likely mean choosing it again and again. But we can trust that God is at work. In them. And in us.

In time—and in God—every hurt can be healed.

God, help me rise above my feelings of anger, outrage, and revenge. I know nothing good can come from these feelings. Instead, give me your peace and focus my mind on your blessings in my life. Help me forgive them because you ask it of me—because you want it for me. Amen.

Digging Deeper

Who do you need to forgive? Ask God to help you let go of the pain so you can choose that forgiveness today.

GOD IS MERCIFUL . . . I AM FORGIVEN

R&R: Rest and Remember

Look back over what you read and wrote this week. What's your main takeaway?

_____

_____

_____

_____

_____

_____

_____

_____

_____

_____

_____

WHAT I CAN DO

GOD IS GOOD . . . I AM BLESSED

May God the Father who made us bless us. May God the Son send his healing among us. May God the Holy Spirit move within us and give us eyes to see with, ears to hear with, and hands that your work might be done. May we walk and preach the world of God to all. May the angel of peace watch over us and lead us at last by God's grace to the Kingdom.

—Prayer of St. Dominic

GOD IS GOOD ... I AM BLESSED

55

You anoint my head with oil; my cup overflows.

—PSALM 23:5

Simply reading Scripture gives us the literal meaning, but God's Word holds so much more. That's why we are encouraged to *pray* with Scripture.

Just reading Scripture is like crunching a hard candy. We get a hint of the taste, but soon it's gone. If we hold that sweet in the pocket of our cheek, however, we savor its real sweetness. It makes the flavor much more intense. In the same way, we *savor* God's Word when we sit with a passage, a line, or sometimes just one word. As we prayerfully hold it in our minds and hearts and think it over, the Holy Spirit helps its richness emerge.

In Psalm 23, we see God as a good shepherd. Spending time with that image helps us understand that God protects us. Encourages us to rest. Even those green pastures come to represent the particular ways God makes us feel safe, secure, and cared for. Later in the psalm, we see God setting a table for us. He's not literally going to make us a PB&J sandwich, but praying with that image shows us that God welcomes us like special guests. He wants to feed our souls and provide for *all* our needs. As we savor these images in prayer, we think about what each means in our lives today.

What do I need from my shepherd? Protection? Rest? Guidance? Ask for his help. *What is my heart hungry for these days? A friend? Reassurance? Hope?* Ask God, knowing he wants to fill you with good things.

The entire psalm—in fact, the entire Bible—shows how God wants to anoint (or bless) us *abundantly* so we have even more than our little cups can hold until it spills over to others in puddles of joy, peace, kindness, hope, and love. "Taste and see that the Lord is good."[1]

Read and savor Scripture. It's what your mind, heart, and spirit crave.

> God, thank you for your Word. Open my eyes, mind, and heart to receive it. To savor its goodness. Help me to understand what you are saying to me through Scripture and to apply it in my life. Amen.

Digging Deeper

1. Read Psalm 23 out loud. Read it slowly and prayerfully. Sit with it and savor it.
2. What words, lines, or images touched your heart? What does that tell you? What might God be telling you through his Word?

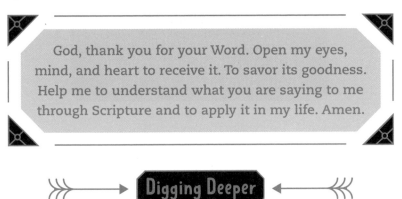

Study your heart in the light of the Holy Scriptures, and you will know therein who you were, who you are, and who you ought to be.

—St. Fulgence of Ruspe

---

1. Psalm 34:8

GOD IS GOOD . . . I AM BLESSED

56

Finally, beloved, whatever is true, whatever is honorable, whatever is just, whatever is pure, whatever is pleasing, whatever is commendable, if there is any excellence and if there is anything worthy of praise, think about these things.

—PHILIPPIANS 4:8

Group work is hard with a pessimist because they see the worst in things. Make a plan and they'll give a hundred reasons why it won't work. Come up with a good idea and they'll shoot it down. Every. Time. Working with someone who only focuses on the negative is draining. We lose our enthusiasm and confidence in the project and, if we aren't careful, find ourselves feeling just as hopeless and helpless.

Now imagine being paired with a pessimist for life! Imagine hearing undermining comments on every decision we make, every word we say, even every thought we have: *Why study? You're going to fail this test.* And *Better not go. Everyone will laugh.* Plus *That's a dumb idea. Keep it to yourself.*

Some of us don't have to imagine it. We listen to negative self-talk without realizing it. We feel down, insecure, and awkward; we dislike ourselves—and don't know why.

God doesn't want us to feel that way. He's eager to pair up

with us on this project called life. With God as our partner, we can make the most of this earthly assignment and create something pretty amazing together. Because God is good, he wants us to be inspired, creative, and excited to make the most of our talents, follow our passions, and live life to the fullest. It's why we're here.

God also wants us to know that we can choose which voice we want to hear loudest: the world's, the enemy's, our insecurities, or God's. We get to pick. Who will you choose?

> God, help me to stop talking negatively to myself and about myself. Show me the brainstorm you have for my life. Help me to see and become that best version of myself. Amen.

Digging Deeper

1. What negative things do you say to or about yourself? Are they really true?
2. List some of those praiseworthy things God gave you. Are you kind? Funny? Thoughtful? Creative? Generous? It gets easier to see them the more often you focus on your blessings. Get in the habit of seeing and celebrating them.

I am inviting you to a dynamic collaboration with God. It is in and through this collaboration that we become the best-version-of-ourselves, in which the loving nature of God is most present.

—MATTHEW KELLY

GOD IS GOOD ... I AM BLESSED

57

> Rejoice always, pray without ceasing, give thanks in all circumstances; for this is the will of God in Christ Jesus for you.

—1 Thessalonians 5:16–18

Your team won. You aced the test. And it's a long weekend. *Life is great.* In moments like these, gratitude wells up and bubbles out and we can't help but think: *God is good! Thanks, God!*

But some days, everything is so . . . *meh.* You missed your bus. You dread another day of boring classes about boring subjects. Even lunch is boring. Or maybe you are having one of *those* days. You got grounded for missing curfew. Your friend is moving away. The teacher kept you after class. And your crush likes someone else. Whatever the struggle—and we all have them—life feels so unfair. When the only thing bubbling up is self-pity, we wallow in it and feel even worse.

Everyone has been there. But we don't have to stay there. In fact, that isn't God's plan for us. St. Paul's advice is to be joyful, prayerful, and thankful in all circumstances.

All circumstances? Easy for him to say. He doesn't know what it's like to be me. Perhaps. But Paul had his own problems. He faced ridicule, hatred, and prejudice as he taught others about Jesus. He was arrested, imprisoned, and eventually killed because of it. But Paul never stopped believing in God's goodness. Even in jail, he kept writing letters encouraging others to believe in Jesus and to praise and thank God.[1] Through it all, Paul's joy, gratitude, and faith did not depend on his situation. They were firmly rooted in the strength and goodness of God.

Life is full of change. There will always be ups and downs, but God is unchanging and ever-present. And he is bigger than any problem. He is with us in all circumstances—blessing, strengthening, and healing us.

> Let nothing disturb you, nothing frighten you; all things are passing; God never changes.
>
> —St. Teresa of Avila

And that's always something to be thankful for.

God, I often let my circumstances determine my mood, and when I'm down I put my energy into complaining and feeling sorry for myself. Help me focus on you—on your goodness, on your power and presence—so at all times, and especially my low moments, I am thankful for all you are and all you do in my life. Amen.

Digging Deeper

1. Think about the past few days. How often have you let your circumstances control your mood and mindset?
2. How might things change for you if you took after St. Paul and rooted your joy, gratitude, and faith in God and not in your situation?

---

1. The New Testament has Paul's letters to: Romans; Corinthians 1&2; Galatians; Ephesians; Philippians; Colossians; Thessalonians 1&2; Timothy 1&2; Titus

58

We know that all things work together for good for those who love God, who are called according to his purpose.

—ROMANS 8:28

Sometimes suffering is due to someone's selfish actions. A person is robbed. A school is vandalized. A student is bullied. But sometimes suffering happens for reasons we can't explain. A child gets cancer. An earthquake destroys. A virus spreads. In those times, we can feel angry, confused, and afraid as we wrestle with BIG questions. *Why did it happen? Where is God?* We may even be tempted to blame God or doubt his goodness. *If God* really *cared, this wouldn't have happened.*

It's important to remember we're in the middle of the story. Often, when we look back, we'll see God's presence, power, and plan. For example, in Genesis, Joseph's brothers sell him into slavery and he ends up in jail. But Joseph never stops trusting God and eventually rises to a position where he saves his family and countless others from famine. In Exodus, Moses leads God's people from slavery to the promised land. While they wander in the desert for *forty long years*, some people question, doubt, and even worship other gods. Yet Moses stays faithful because he *remembers* what God has already done and trusts him. In the Gospels, Mary stands by the cross watching her son die. Yet even in her grief, her faith never wavered.

None of these people faced their problem alone. They may not have fully understood *why* but they completely trusted *who*. They trusted in God's goodness, wisdom, and greater plan.

As we get tossed around by challenges in life, it's important to anchor ourselves in God's Word to remind ourselves that he *does* care. God loves us, *deeply*. God is with us, *always*. And that even if we can't make sense of things right now, *God has a plan*.

God can—and will—bring good from all things. Trust him.

> Whatever good or evil befalls you, be confident that God will convert it all to your good.
>
> —St. Jane Frances de Chantal

God, I struggle to make sense of suffering and evil in the world. Help me remember I won't always understand *why* things happen, but my heart can trust in your greater plan to bring about good from every circumstance. Amen.

Digging Deeper

1. Write down this prayer and read it regularly:

   God, grant me the serenity to accept the things I cannot change; courage to change the things I can; and wisdom to know the difference.

   —Serenity Prayer

2. How do these words apply to your life right now?

59

> The thief comes only to steal and kill and destroy. I came that they might have life, and have it abundantly.
>
> —JOHN 10:10

Jesus tells us that God wants to bless us *abundantly*. But often we miss those blessings because of a thief. Jesus himself tells us that the enemy wants to steal from us; to take our joy, hope, and love for God and others. The enemy tries to spoil all that is good and right and true by stirring our anxiety, sowing seeds of doubt, and fueling our fear. How? He lies.

Those lies influenced Adam and Eve to doubt God and God's goodness, even when they were surrounded by it in the garden of Eden. The enemy even tried to tempt Jesus in the desert but Jesus stayed strong in God's Word. Today, this enemy is still present and just as sneaky. He may not be tempting us to pick fruit or turn stones to bread, but he'll point out all that is wrong with our lives so we think we aren't blessed. He'll highlight all that is wrong with us so we think we aren't good. And when we are feeling down and alone, the enemy will try to convince us that we don't matter, that nobody cares about us. Not even God.

But they're all tricks. Because the truth is, we *are* blessed—abundantly. We're God's beloved kids. And God is constantly sending us signs to show how much we mean to him, how special we are, how close he is. As we pay attention to God's truth in his Word and in our hearts, we'll start to notice more of the countless large and small ways God blesses us. That moment of calm when things are crazy. That sense of what's right in the midst of con-fusion. A stranger's smile, a random quote, or friend reaching out when we need it most.

It's all God's help: his grace. It's all God's blessing.

We need to start looking

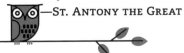

> When you lie down on your bed, remember with thanksgiving the blessings and the providence of God.
> —St. Antony the Great

for God's blessings sent through the people, places, and things in everyday life. As we do, we will discover that we are even more blessed than we could have imagined.

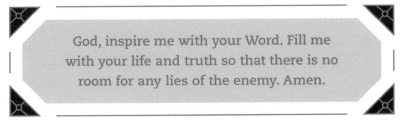

God, inspire me with your Word. Fill me with your life and truth so that there is no room for any lies of the enemy. Amen.

Digging Deeper

1. Each night before you fall asleep, remember your blessings. Recall the many good things of that day and thank God for them.
2. When tempted, Jesus responds with Scripture, and we can do the same. What are your favorite verses? If you can't remember any, look back through this book and pick your top three. Write each down and memorize them.

GOD IS GOOD ... I AM BLESSED

60

Ask and it will be given to you; search, and you will find; knock, and the door will be opened for you.

—MATTHEW 7:7

Ask, search, and knock—and we will receive. We can count on that promise. "Is there anyone among you who, if your child asks for bread, will give a stone?" Jesus adds.[1] Everyone knows any good parent is going to provide what their kids need. To feed them when they're hungry. To clothe them. To shelter them. Why? Because they love them. Jesus says that if people—who aren't perfect—know how to give good things to their kids, "how much more will your Father in heaven give good things to those who ask him!"[2]

God is all good, totally loving, and extravagantly generous. But that doesn't mean we get *everything* we want *when* we want it just because we want it. Why? Because he loves us.

If a toddler wanted candy for dinner every night, should she get it? What if she really wanted to play with that shiny, sharp knife? Would you let her drive the car if she threw a tantrum about it? Sometimes, what we want isn't what we really need. Other times, what we think we want can actually be bad for us. And a lot of the time God's answer is *not yet*.

---

1. Matthew 7:9
2. Matthew 7:11

As we wait in faith, we learn to be patient. We trust in God's perfect timing knowing he will give us exactly what we need when we need it.

Whatever we ask for in prayer, above all we trust in God's wisdom and love. God knows far more than us and is always thinking of our good.

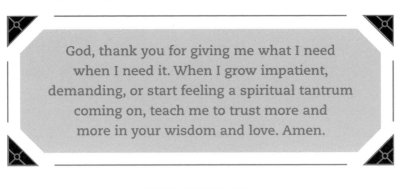

God, thank you for giving me what I need when I need it. When I grow impatient, demanding, or start feeling a spiritual tantrum coming on, teach me to trust more and more in your wisdom and love. Amen.

Digging Deeper

What unanswered prayer do you carry in your heart? Talk to God about it. Ask him for his wisdom and strength as you wait, trusting in God's timing and plan.

> To be grateful is to recognize the love of God in everything he has given us—and he has given us everything.
>
> —THOMAS MERTON

GOD IS GOOD . . . I AM BLESSED

R&R: Rest and Remember

Look back over what you read and wrote this week. What's your main takeaway?

_____

_____

_____

_____

_____

_____

_____

_____

_____

_____

_____

WHAT I CAN DO

GOD IS POWERFUL . . . I AM STRONG

Lord, give me light, that I may see your way.
Lord, give me strength, that I may follow your way.
Lord, give me love, that I may do your will.

—FROM THE NOVENA TO ST. WALBURGA

GOD IS POWERFUL... I AM STRONG

61

> Be strong and courageous; do not be frightened or dismayed, for the Lord your God is with you wherever you go.
>
> —JOSHUA 1:9

Everyone knows Moses.[1] He's the guy who led God's people out of slavery in Egypt, parted the Red Sea, and hung out with God on mountaintops. For forty years, the Israelites followed their leader Moses and, as God promised, Moses led them to the promised land. Then, just as they were about to cross over the river and onto the land, Moses died of old age. But what was it like to be Joshua, the guy left in charge? I mean, Moses left some pretty big sandals to fill. Did Joshua, his second in command, feel ready to take over as leader? Did he worry about letting people down? Was he afraid he'd never be able to lead like Moses?

A lot of Bible stories show people hearing God's call and doubting themselves. Even Moses first wondered, *Me, God? Are you sure?* But God promised Moses he would be with him. And God was. God promised to be with Joshua. And God was. God promised to be with Mary. And God was. Today, God promises to be with us. And he is.

---

1. If you're not familiar, you can find his story in the book of Exodus.

Because God never breaks a promise.

God promises to be with us, to equip us. He promises to strengthen us so we can do his will; accomplish amazing things we may have never thought possible. God gives us wisdom and words. He gives us courage and confidence.

What Moses, Joshua, Mary, and every faith-filled person since has learned is that it doesn't really matter what we think we can't do. What really matters is that we trust in what God *can* and *will* do. If we focus less on our weaknesses—and more on God's strengths—we will see that God is faithful, trustworthy, and strong.

He will never let us down.

> **Pray as though everything depended on God. Work as though everything depended on you.**
> —ATTRIBUTED TO ST. IGNATIUS OF LOYOLA

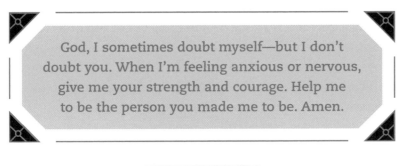

God, I sometimes doubt myself—but I don't doubt you. When I'm feeling anxious or nervous, give me your strength and courage. Help me to be the person you made me to be. Amen.

Digging Deeper

1. What doubts do you have about saying yes to God's call?
2. Are you relying on your strength . . . or his?

GOD IS POWERFUL . . . I AM STRONG

62

> I write to you, young people, because you are strong and the word of God abides in you, and you have overcome the evil one.

—1 John 2:14

Some little kids are afraid of the dark. Others are convinced monsters are lurking in their closet or hiding under their bed. Those anxieties may seem silly to us now, but for us at that age, they felt real. We couldn't hop out of bed and turn on the light. We couldn't open the closet or look under the bed to prove nothing was there. Fear wouldn't let us risk it. So instead of facing our fears, we'd lie there imagining the worst-case scenario—feeling more and more terrified.

In some ways, we're still trapped by fear. Our dark corners and closet monsters come in different forms these days— failure, rejection, self-doubt—but make no mistake, they are just as scary. The truth is, everyone fears failure. We've fallen short in the past, we know how it feels to fail, and we don't ever want to risk feeling like that again. As a result, we convince ourselves not to try, and stay stuck where we are—like that scared, little kid hiding under a blanket—paralyzed by fear.

God wants to free us from all fear. He wants to turn on the light and show us the truth about who we are, what we can do, and the help we have in him. With God, we can push past those doubts and move from a fearful *what if* to a fearless *why not!* Try out for that team. Present that project. Go introduce yourself to that new friend. Because living, loving, and learning is always worth the risk.

We are stronger, braver, and wiser than we think—because God is with us. He's in us. God's power and presence make us more resilient too. That means that even if we fall short—and we still will from time to time—God will give us the strength to get up and try again. To keep going. To keep moving forward. Bravely.

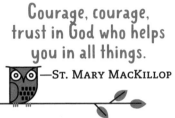

Courage, courage, trust in God who helps you in all things.

—St. Mary MacKillop

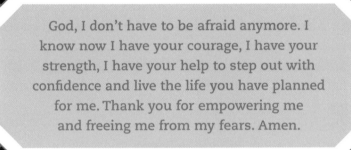

God, I don't have to be afraid anymore. I know now I have your courage, I have your strength, I have your help to step out with confidence and live the life you have planned for me. Thank you for empowering me and freeing me from my fears. Amen.

Digging Deeper

1. What fears hold you back from being all that you can? Rejection? Ridicule? Failure? Perfectionism? Talk to God about it. Ask him to free you from that fear and give you the courage to step out in faith.
2. Make a plan with God to take one small, brave step forward this week.

GOD IS POWERFUL . . . I AM STRONG

63

I can do all things through him who strengthens me.

—PHILIPPIANS 4:13

Any athlete will tell you that strength doesn't happen overnight. It takes training and practice. It takes continuous effort, commitment, and time. In the beginning, it doesn't seem like lifting weights, stretching, or doing push-ups makes any difference at all. But each run and every rep helps to strengthen and build that muscle bit by bit. In time, we see results.

The same is true for spiritual strength—it takes daily commitment and effort. But the only way to develop it—the reps we need to do—is to rely more and more on God. It's kind of ironic, actually, because spiritual strength can only happen if we first admit our total weakness. It means facing and accepting the truth: *I don't have enough courage, faith, wisdom, patience, endurance . . . or whatever this particular situation needs. I just don't have it.*

But God does. And the more we accept that we don't know all the answers, that we aren't in control, and that we are pretty much hopeless without God's help, the more we come to rely on him. The fact is, the sooner we stop being full of ourselves, the sooner God's strength can and will fill us.

That's what it means to be humble. Humility isn't

something our world tends to admire because it seems to go against today's attention-seeking drive to get the most likes, praise, and attention. We can be a self-centric person, but honestly, despite all the so-called likes, does anyone *really* like that?

Know who you *really* are. Be *that* person. And be okay with all you can't do. Because as long as you seek to know who God is too, he is going to give you the strength you need to do all kinds of amazing things.

> God, I am nothing without you. I need you in my life, even when I think I have it all covered. Especially then. Be my personal trainer, God. Strengthen me, in mind and spirit. Rep by rep, day by day. Amen.

Digging Deeper

1. When have you felt God's strength in the midst of your weakness?
2. When were you able to draw upon God's strength (his patience, wisdom, insight, peacefulness, etc.) that you didn't know you had?

> If you should ask me what are the ways of God, I would tell you that the first is humility, the second is humility, and the third is still humility . . . If humility does not precede all that we do, our efforts are fruitless.
>
> —St. Augustine

GOD IS POWERFUL... I AM STRONG

64

Resist the devil and he will flee from you.

—JAMES 4:7

Do you keep promises? Are you truthful? Do you share juicy gossip? Temptation comes in many forms and we all face it.

Even Jesus. After he spent forty days fasting in the desert, the enemy believed Jesus was weak, alone, and hungry and tried to tempt him. He wanted Jesus to give up his fast. He wanted Jesus to give in to hopelessness and doubt if God the Father really cared about him. And finally, the enemy promised power and fame if Jesus worshiped him instead of God.

How did Jesus respond to these temptations and lies? With the truth of God's Word. And by doing so, Jesus showed us we can do it too.[1]

We won't be tempted to turn stones to bread, but the enemy tempts us in specific ways that we hunger after. *Want to be more popular? Want to get even? Just take and do whatever you want—why shouldn't you?*

The enemy wants us to give in to our selfish wants—our greed, pride, anger, envy, lust, and laziness—and to give up on what we know is right and good. He stirs that hunger and the random thoughts that say: *Just take it. Just do it. Just say it.* Soon, we can even convince ourselves we *deserve* whatever we want.

---

1. Read about Jesus facing and overcoming temptation in Matthew 4:1–11

But every sinful choice weakens us. It hurts us and others. Ultimately, sin drags us farther and farther from God and from being the good, loving, and joyful person we were meant to be. That's exactly what the enemy wants.

Don't give in to temptation. Don't believe the lies and false promises. Instead, when you notice you are being tempted—reach for God and rely on his strength. Remember God's truth, and, like Jesus, speak God's Word.

Because the best way to dispel the darkness is simply to turn on the light.

> God, when I am feeling weak and tempted to sin, nudge my conscience. Make me aware of the choices before me. Give me the strength to choose you and to do the right thing. Amen.

Digging Deeper

1. When have you felt the Holy Spirit nudging your conscience? What was he urging you to do? Did you do it?
2. The more we respond to the nudging of the Holy Spirit, the easier it becomes to sense it next time. Talk to the Holy Spirit. Ask him to help you stay strong when you are tempted again.

Above all, we must be especially alert against the beginnings of temptation, for the enemy is more easily conquered if he is refused admittance to the mind and is met beyond the threshold when he knocks.

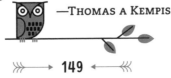
—THOMAS A KEMPIS

GOD IS POWERFUL... I AM STRONG

65

> Finally, be strong in the Lord and in the strength of his power. Put on the whole armor of God, so that you may be able to stand against the wiles of the devil.

—EPHESIANS 6:10–11

Your favorite team is in the Super Bowl. But as the players line up on the scrimmage line to start the game, you suddenly notice that *none* of them are wearing *any* protective gear. No shoulder pads. No cleats. No mouth guards. Not even one helmet.

Your heart sinks. Without the right equipment, your team can't possibly be as strong, confident, or skilled. They'll be easily defeated and probably get injured in the very first tackle.

Only a fool plays full contact football without the proper equipment! And yet, that's how many of us live our lives.

God has given us all the equipment we need to be strong, confident, and skilled—such as wisdom to make good decisions, courage to face our fears, endurance to persevere. It's everything we need to be victorious, no matter how dirty the enemy plays. But it's up to us to use it.

St. Paul encourages us all to "put on the whole armor

of God."[1] He also tell us: "Clothe yourselves with compassion, kindness, humility, meekness, and patience . . . Above all, clothe yourselves with love, which binds everything together in perfect harmony."[2]

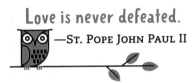

Love is never defeated.
—ST. POPE JOHN PAUL II

So suit up in God's truth, righteousness, peace, faith, and love and stand firm against any play the devil makes. Block any temptation. Intercept every lie. Because when we commit to God's team, and use the plans and equipment God gives us, we don't just win against the enemy—it's a total blowout.

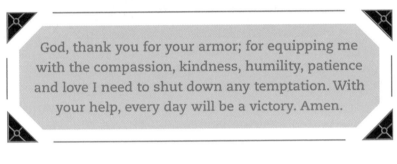

God, thank you for your armor; for equipping me with the compassion, kindness, humility, patience and love I need to shut down any temptation. With your help, every day will be a victory. Amen.

Digging Deeper

1. Read Ephesians 6:11–17 and make a list of every piece of the armor of God.
2. Read Colossians 3:12–17 and add the virtues we should put on to your list.
3. Put a star beside the ones you most need today as a reminder to gear up.

---

1. Ephesians 6:11
2. Colossians 3:12,14

GOD IS POWERFUL... I AM STRONG

66

> I pray that, according to the riches of his glory, he may grant that you may be strengthened in your inner being with power through his Spirit.
>
> —EPHESIANS 3:16

Core strengthening stabilizes our spine, gives us good posture and balance, and prevents injuries. A solid core affects the health of the entire body. But rock-hard abs aren't the inner strength this passage is talking about. That powerful inner strength only comes from God's Spirit at work in us.

The Holy Spirit wants to transform us. He's like a personal trainer for our spiritual selves. He wants to guide us and help strengthen us to develop in character and virtue; to become more loving, more kind, generous, and patient, more faithful, peaceful, and joyful. Ultimately, the Holy Spirit wants to help us to become more loving.

More like Jesus.

And our wonderful trainer does more than just coach, because the Holy Spirit actually *empowers* us. Just by having him with us, we are *already* a bit stronger, wiser, kinder, and more loving. And any time we feel tempted to give up, give in, or give out, all we have to do is call on the Holy Spirit and he is there, ready to give us a boost in whatever way we need.

God's Spirit inspires and creates, he renews and restores,

he brings faith, hope, and love and grace after grace. He keeps us energized and balanced. Healthy and strong. When we have the Holy Spirit at work in our core—in the deepest part of who we are—he strengthens us. He transforms our spirits. And through each one of us he strengthens and transforms our world.

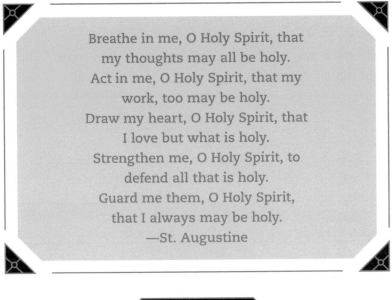

Breathe in me, O Holy Spirit, that
my thoughts may all be holy.
Act in me, O Holy Spirit, that my
work, too may be holy.
Draw my heart, O Holy Spirit, that
I love but what is holy.
Strengthen me, O Holy Spirit, to
defend all that is holy.
Guard me them, O Holy Spirit,
that I always may be holy.
—St. Augustine

Digging Deeper

Write this simple and powerful prayer in your journal or somewhere you can read it often.

GOD IS POWERFUL . . . I AM STRONG

R&R: Rest and Remember

Look back over what you read and wrote this week. What's your main takeaway?

_____

_____

_____

_____

_____

_____

_____

_____

_____

_____

WHAT I CAN DO

GOD IS GENEROUS . . . I AM GIFTED

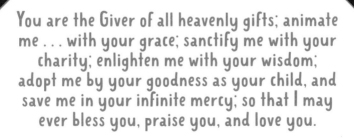

You are the Giver of all heavenly gifts; animate me . . . with your grace; sanctify me with your charity; enlighten me with your wisdom; adopt me by your goodness as your child, and save me in your infinite mercy; so that I may ever bless you, praise you, and love you.

—FROM "PRAYER TO THE HOLY SPIRIT"
BY ST. ALPHONSUS LIGUORI

GOD IS GENEROUS . . . I AM GIFTED

67

> But we have this treasure in clay jars, so that it may be made clear that this extraordinary power belongs to God and does not come from us.
>
> —2 CORINTHIANS 4:7

Are you gifted?

"Who, me?" most of us would laugh and sarcastically answer. "Yeah, right. Oh, I'm just *so amazing*."

We tend to think that being gifted means we are exceptional. We assume a gifted person does amazing things. So if we aren't one of those top performers in academics, sports, art, music, or whatever, we figure the term *gifted* doesn't apply to us. But the truth is, giftedness isn't based on our performance or ability. *Gifted* just means that we have been "given a gift." And we have. In fact, we've been given many gifts.

God has given each of us our own unique combination of natural abilities, talents, and strengths. It's that treasure inside of us. Just because someone else can do something as well, or maybe better, than us right now doesn't mean that skill isn't part of our gift. That's like saying a bulb, sprout, or bud isn't really a tulip. It may not be a full-blown blossom yet—but in every stage, it's all tulip.

It's the same with our gifts. Some are well-developed. We might already know we rock at sports or problem solving. But other gifts are still germinating underground. We might have the gifts for being an understanding parent, a loving spouse, or a compassionate doctor—but don't know it yet. These gifts won't be fully revealed until the season of our life when we need them.

God gifts us according to his plan for our lives. He equips and empowers us with what we need at every stage of life to be the person he designed. So don't bother comparing your gifts to others'.

Small vessels may hold great gifts.

—St. Ephraem
the Syrian

Each of us is uniquely gifted for our own unique life and purpose. And each of us is a jar brimming with treasures just waiting to be discovered.

Now *that* sounds pretty amazing, doesn't it?

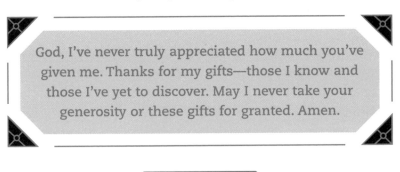

God, I've never truly appreciated how much you've given me. Thanks for my gifts—those I know and those I've yet to discover. May I never take your generosity or these gifts for granted. Amen.

Digging Deeper

1. What are your natural abilities, talents, and strengths? Thank God for them.
2. What gifts do you think might be germinating in you? Ask God to help you to discover them and nurture them.

GOD IS GENEROUS . . . I AM GIFTED

68

Now there are varieties of gifts, but the same Spirit; and there are varieties of services, but the same Lord; and there are varieties of activities, but it is the same God who activates all of them in everyone.

—1 CORINTHIANS 12:4–6

I t's true that being athletic, smart, artistic, and musical are gifts. But they aren't the *only* gifts; they're simply the ones that are often recognized and celebrated. School is a clear example of that. We are marked on how well we can read, write, and repeat what we've learned on a test. We are graded on how well we can run the track, shoot a free throw, or hit a baseball in gym class. Our report cards tell us how well, or how poorly, we did on mastering a specific skillset in a specific subject over a specific time period.

But that isn't *all* that we are. It isn't *who* we are.

If we do well at school, we can be proud of our achievements, but being an honor student only means we are good at those specific skills. It doesn't make us superior. It doesn't mean we are better than someone who barely passes. In the same way, if we do poorly at school, it doesn't mean we are dumb or not good at anything. Many successful adults struggled in school but later discovered their true strengths and gifts in new areas.

The point is, we are all gifted in ways that never appear on a report card. What about kindness? That's a gift. What about generosity? Or being thoughtful and inspiring? What about the way we always make people laugh, how people feel so at ease around us, or the fact our friends like to confide in us? Joy, hospitality, empathy, compassion—just imagine a world without them.

If you are what you should be, you will set the whole world on fire!

—ST. CATHERINE OF SIENNA

God is a generous giver. He longs to lavish us with a wide variety of gifts. Some are academic. Some are athletic. Some are creative. But many are a part of being a good, loving, joyful person.

And those are often what the world needs most.

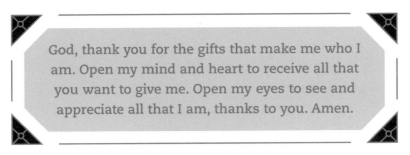

God, thank you for the gifts that make me who I am. Open my mind and heart to receive all that you want to give me. Open my eyes to see and appreciate all that I am, thanks to you. Amen.

Digging Deeper

1. How much of your identity and self-worth comes from your marks at school? Do you label others or treat them differently based on their grades?
2. What are some of your gifts and your friends' gifts that never appear on a report card? Thank God for those. Celebrate those. And share those gifts as much as you can.

69

> I am the vine, you are the branches.
> Those who abide in me and I in them
> bear much fruit, because apart
> from me you can do nothing.

—JOHN 15:5

God has given each of us many wonderful gifts, but they don't arrive fully formed. Most of our gifts take effort to discover and develop. It's kind of like growing fruit. Grapes, for example, don't suddenly appear on the vine. They take effort as the gardener tends, weeds, waters, and prunes the vine. But in time, and in the right season, those bare branches will bear lots of fruit.

So how do we know what gifts might be sprouting in us? We look at our personalities and passions. For example, what is something people notice about you? What word would they use to describe you?

Maybe you cry at sad books and movies. You worry about other people's problems as if they are your own. People say you're "too sensitive." But with a little tending, that might be the gift of compassion. Or maybe you are the kind of person who always tells others what to do and when to do it. You like to take charge, and people might accuse you of being "too bossy." But what if that is really the budding gift of leadership? Or maybe you are a daydreamer. You find it hard to pay attention in class or even in conversations because your mind keeps wandering. People say you're "too distracted." But you may actually be growing the gifts of wonder and imagination.

Early on, our gifts might be misunderstood as something else—even as a weakness. But they aren't. Just as those branches of small grapes need to stay rooted in the vine to grow, we need to stay rooted in Jesus and nurtured by the Spirit. God will help us get rid of all the bitter parts of ourselves and help us develop our gifts into something wonderful and sweet.

> God, I don't really know my gifts yet, but it helps to know they are there, growing and maturing as I do. As I stay rooted in you, help my gifts to become clearer to me and helpful to others. Amen.

Digging Deeper

1. What words would your friends, parents, teachers, coaches, or classmates use to describe you? Brainstorm as many as you can.
2. Do these descriptions hint at your developing gifts?

God wants you to be yourself. But not the self your ego wants you to be, and not the self the world wants you to be. Rather the self God had in mind when he created you. By calling you to live an authentic life, God is saying, "Be all I create you to be."

—MATTHEW KELLY

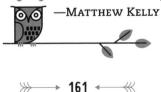

70

Like good stewards of the manifold grace of God, serve one another with whatever gift each of you has received.

—1 PETER 4:10

Admit it. It feels good to score that winning goal. To ace the test our friends barely passed. To draw, build, or play something others totally admire. As we grow and develop our strengths, we'll start to notice there are things we can do that others cannot no matter how much they practice. But our strengths can become our weaknesses if we aren't careful.

Maybe we start doing those things *for* the recognition and praise. Or maybe we talk about our great accomplishments just a little too much. Or, worse yet, we use those abilities to make ourselves feel bigger and better by making others feel small.

Pride is not God's plan. Not at all. He wants us to use our gifts and do what we do best. That's why he gave them to us. But he always wants us to remember it's a *gift*. The fact God gave it to us to use and develop should make us grateful to him, not boastful about it.

God also wants us to use our gifts for the good of all. In fact, he gives us the tools we need to build good things in our world as we work *together*. That's why we all have *different* gifts to contribute. What good is a toolbox full of identical hammers? A hammer can't saw wood or sand edges or tighten a bolt. But it can do what it was perfectly designed to do: hammer nails. In the same way, our world needs our variety of gifts. One gift is no better than another. All are necessary. And each serves its specific purpose in the Master Builder's plan.

> Take, Lord, and receive all my liberty, my memory, my understanding, and my entire will. All I have and call my own. You have given all to me. To you, Lord, I return it. Everything is yours; do with it what you will. Give me only your love and your grace, that is enough for me.
> —St. Ignatius of Loyola

1. When it comes to your gifts—are you boastful or grateful?
2. Do you seek the praise of others or speak your thanks to God?

GOD IS GENEROUS...I AM GIFTED

71

> And God is able to provide you with every blessing in abundance, so that by always having enough of everything, you may share abundantly in every good work.
>
> —2 CORINTHIANS 9:8

In almost every adventure story, some wise and usually elder mentor helps to train the hero for the journey ahead. The hero may feel unworthy or unready, but the mentor sees the hero's potential and inspires them to work and train hard, while also helping the hero become strong. Just before the hero finally sets out on his quest, the mentor gives him a special gift. It might be a sword or lightsaber. It could be a magical map, ruby slippers, or some sage words. Whatever it is, in the challenge ahead, that gift will be *exactly* what the hero needed.

Wouldn't it be great to have a mentor like that? Someone who sees our potential when others can't. Someone who believes in us when others don't. Someone willing to put in the time and effort it takes to teach us and train us so that we become even better than we'd ever imagined.

The truth is, we do have a mentor like that. Each of us have unlimited access to the most *powerful*, most *wise*, and most *generous* mentor of all: God.

Think about that for a second. The all-powerful, all-knowing, ever-present creator of the entire universe wants to mentor you. He wants to train you and help you develop amazing skills. He wants to work in you and with you to make you stronger. God knows exactly what you will need for the adventures ahead and he wants to give it to you. *Abundantly!*

Unlike all the other mentors who leave the hero to go it alone, our almighty mentor wants to be part of our stories, in every chapter of our lives.

And with him by our side, our lives will be epic!

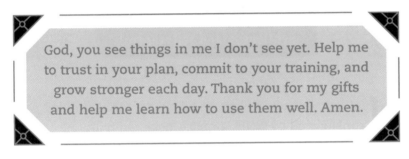

God, you see things in me I don't see yet. Help me to trust in your plan, commit to your training, and grow stronger each day. Thank you for my gifts and help me learn how to use them well. Amen.

Digging Deeper

1. What area of your life could use a mentor's help? What makes you feel anxious?
2. Ask God to help prepare and equip you. Ask him for the courage to rise to the challenge.

God did not tell us to follow him because he needed our help, but because he knew that loving him would make us whole.

—St. Irenaeus

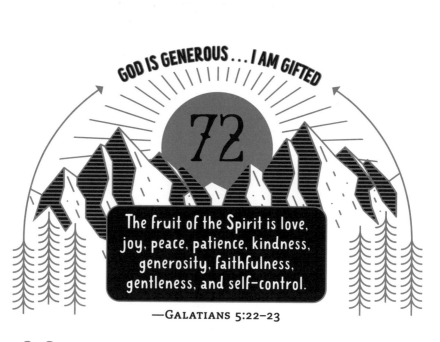

GOD IS GENEROUS ... I AM GIFTED

72

The fruit of the Spirit is love, joy, peace, patience, kindness, generosity, faithfulness, gentleness, and self-control.

—GALATIANS 5:22–23

Want to know how well we're being mentored, molded, and transformed by God? Simple. Check the fruit!

The more God's Spirit works within us, the more fruit of the Spirit we'll see. We'll be patient even when things are irritating. Instead of being greedy, we'll be more generous with what we have. When good things happen to someone else, we'll be truly happy for them instead of feeling envious. We'll feel more peaceful and not take everything personally. We'll know how to control our wants instead of letting them control us. We'll have solid faith and never doubt. And we'll always feel a deep sense of joy no matter what is happening.

Sounds almost impossible, doesn't it?

Well, it would be if we were trying to achieve all those things on our own. Thankfully, we have the Spirit's help. The more we allow the Holy Spirit to work in us, the more fruitful we naturally become.

We know trees by their fruit. Apple trees grow apples. Orange trees produce oranges. As a follower of Jesus, we're also known by our fruit. Like Jesus said: "Everyone will know

that you are my disciples, if you have love for one another."[1]
So ask God for help to be more loving, more joyful, peaceful, patient, and kind. Whatever the fruit, if we draw near to God and open wide our hearts, in time God will provide.

He always makes good things grow.

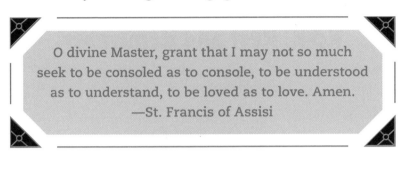

O divine Master, grant that I may not so much seek to be consoled as to console, to be understood as to understand, to be loved as to love. Amen.
—St. Francis of Assisi

Digging Deeper

1. What weaknesses do you need help with? Ask God to cultivate more of the fruit of the Spirit in you. Be specific about which ones you most desire in this season of your life.
2. What fruit are you already seeing in yourself?

> The fruit silence is prayer; the fruit of prayer is faith; the fruit of faith is love; the fruit of love is service; the fruit of service is peace.
> —St. Teresa of Calcutta

---

1. John 13:35

GOD IS GENEROUS . . . I AM GIFTED

R&R: Rest and Remember

Look back over what you read and wrote this week. What's your main takeaway?

_____

_____

_____

_____

_____

_____

_____

_____

_____

_____

WHY I CAN DO IT

GOD IS CALLING . . . I AM CALLED

My Lord God, I have no idea where I am going. I do not see the road ahead of me . . . But I believe that the desire to please you does in fact please you. And I hope I have that desire in all that I am doing. I hope that I will never do anything apart from that desire. And I know that, if I do this, you will lead me by the right road, though I may know nothing about it. Therefore I will trust you always . . .
Amen.

—THOMAS MERTON

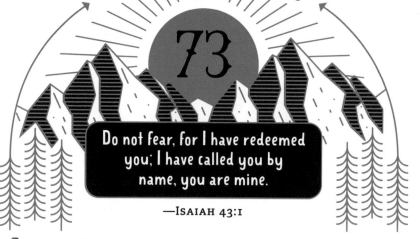

GOD IS CALLING... I AM CALLED

73

> Do not fear, for I have redeemed you; I have called you by name, you are mine.

—Isaiah 43:1

If you got lost downtown and a random stranger called you over and started giving you directions home, you'd probably ignore them. Even if the route sounded easy, you wouldn't take it. Why? Because this guy doesn't even know you or where you live. Why would you trust him?

But if you got a call from Mom or Dad with directions home—you'd listen. Even if the route sounded really long and complex, you'd still take it. Why? Because you *know* them. You know they love you. You know they want to help you find your way to where they are. Because of what you know about them, because of your relationship, you trust them.

Why not listen to God with that same confidence? God knows you better than you even know yourself. He loves you more than anyone else ever has or will. God is calling you and he has a wonderful plan and purpose for you.

Why wander lost and confused? When you are at a crossroads and don't know what to do; when you feel anxious about the future; when you doubt yourself—ask God for direction. Tell him where you are and where you hope to be. Listen for

his nudge in your heart and in his Word and then step out in faith. If you trust him, God will lead you exactly where you are meant to be.

> God, sometimes my wandering leads me away from you. When I feel lost and anxious, remind me that you are with me. Always. I trust in your love and wisdom. Show me the way. Amen.

1. What makes you feel anxious about the future?
2. In what ways have you felt lost lately? Talk to God about it.

God leads every soul
by a unique path.
—St. John of the Cross

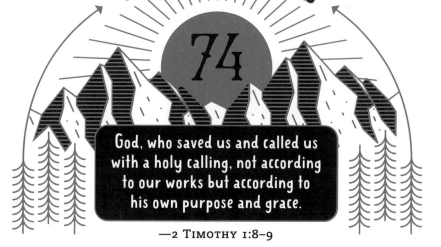

GOD IS CALLING . . . I AM CALLED

74

God, who saved us and called us with a holy calling, not according to our works but according to his own purpose and grace.

—2 TIMOTHY 1:8–9

The gym teacher announces we're playing football today. Everyone lines up as the two captains take turns picking their players. One by one, the teams start to take shape. Finally, we hear our name called and—relieved—we head over, excited to join our team. It feels good to be chosen. We like to be noticed and wanted for what we bring to a group, and being selected gives us a sense of belonging and ability. But being called on doesn't just happen in gym class.

God calls each of us every day of our lives. He wants us on his team.

Seems incredible, doesn't it? I mean, if God could have anyone, why would he want *us*? We're no superstar saints. We make mistakes, and lots of them. Honestly, we're total rookies, just learning as we go.

But God still wants us.

He calls each of us by name. Asking us to come closer to him; to listen up and tune in to his coaching. He wants to inspire us to dig deeper and try harder so we grow in spiritual strength. Yes, we'll drop the ball countless times, but God wants us to learn from our fumbles and keep going when we'd rather just quit. That development is how we learn and how we change. As we follow God's plays and his plans for us, we become the MVPs God knows each of us can be.

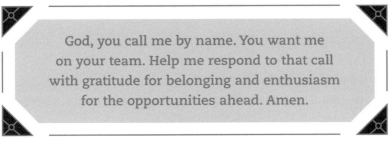

May you trust God that you are exactly where you are meant to be.

—St. Thérèse of Lisieux

We might doubt our abilities from time to time. We may question why he wants us. Or wonder if we'll ever be good enough—but we never have to doubt God. Only God knows the perfect plan for someone with our strengths. We can trust him. Completely.

God, you call me by name. You want me on your team. Help me respond to that call with gratitude for belonging and enthusiasm for the opportunities ahead. Amen.

Digging Deeper

1. God knows you best and still calls you to do his work right where you are. In what ways do you feel God is calling you?
2. What do you bring to his team?

GOD IS CALLING . . . I AM CALLED

75

Then I heard the voice of the Lord saying, "Whom shall I send, and who will go for us?" And I said, "Here am I; send me!"

—ISAIAH 6:8

If the doorbell rings, a friend texts, or the teacher calls our name, we answer. We respond to calls all the time. But how do we respond to God's call?

In this Scripture passage, Isaiah shows us. It's also how Moses replied. Mary and countless others in Scripture answer God's call with the same three words: *Here I am.*

It's a simple response with a profound meaning. It shows God we hear him. It shows we are present and attentive. Most of all, it shows we are ready and willing to do God's will. We may not know what he wants us to do, how we'll do it, or even for whom—yet. But none of that matters. Those biblical heroes didn't have all the answers when they said yes either. Abraham was old and childless when God called him to be a father to the nations. Moses was starting a new life after escaping Egypt when God called him to go back and lead the Israelites to freedom. And Mary was a small-town, teenaged girl whose greatest hope was to marry Joseph when God called her to be the mother of his Son. No doubt, they had lots of questions.

But they didn't need to know the how, why, when, or where—because they knew the *who*. They completely trusted God would help them do whatever he asked. As the saying goes: God doesn't call the prepared, he prepares the called. And God did equip and strengthen them. He was with them through it all. All they had to do was show up and then keep showing up to God's call on their lives.

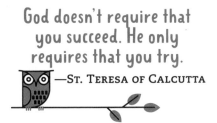

God doesn't require that you succeed. He only requires that you try.

—St. Teresa of Calcutta

God doesn't expect us to have all the answers or know the whole plan. He has all that covered. His hope is we hear his call and show up. Ready. Willing. And open as we say: *Here I am.*

God, I realize now I don't need to have all the answers to answer your call. I know you have a plan. I trust in it because I trust in you. Help me to start each day, each conversation, each action and interaction with a heart set on you and on doing your will: *Here I am.* Amen.

Digging Deeper

1. Write the words *Here I am.* Then continue with what you want to say to God right now. If nothing comes to mind, write what you think God wants to let you know.
2. There are many long and wonderful prayers, but for the next week, try starting your day with one that is three simple words: *Here I am.* Then sit in silence with God and listen for how he might be nudging your heart.

Train yourself in godliness, for, while physical training is of some value, godliness is valuable in every way, holding promise for both the present life and the life to come.

—1 TIMOTHY 4:7–8

It's when we know we should probably get up and help bring in the groceries . . . *but* our favorite show is on. It's when we suddenly get an idea for something that would cheer up a friend . . . *but* instead of taking action, we think of all the reasons it probably won't work. It's when we had the best intentions to spend time with God . . . *but* somehow the plans fell through. Again. *I'll do it later. Tomorrow. Maybe.*

The more we hear God's call or feel the nudge of the Holy Spirit and ignore it, the more we risk becoming the spiritual version of a couch potato. You know, the kind that just laze around doing *nothing* for so long that they become overwhelmed at the thought of doing *anything*. Much like our physical selves, our spiritual selves grow lethargic and weaker the less we use those muscles. Eventually, we can actually become numb and deaf to God's call.

Thankfully, the opposite is also true.

Athletes may not *feel* like exercising, but they know a little exercise every day makes a big difference in their overall performance and strength, so they choose to train. In the same way, we may not *feel* like praying, but we choose to begin. We may not *feel* like helping, but we decide to take that first step. Each time we do, God gives us the grace to keep going and we grow stronger and stronger. And just like the more we exercise a muscle, the stronger it gets, the more often we are kind—the kinder we become. The more we do thoughtful things—the more thoughtful we become. Even forgiving others comes easier the more often we do it.

We grow stronger or weaker one *choice* at a time. Choose wisely.

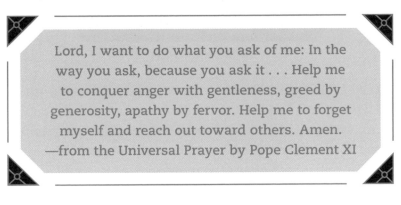

Lord, I want to do what you ask of me: In the way you ask, because you ask it . . . Help me to conquer anger with gentleness, greed by generosity, apathy by fervor. Help me to forget myself and reach out toward others. Amen.
—from the Universal Prayer by Pope Clement XI

Digging Deeper

1. Recall a recent time you felt the nudge to do good and ignored it. How did that make you feel?
2. What might have happened if you had acted instead?
3. How might God be nudging you today? Take that first step, and know that he will help you keep growing stronger.

GOD IS CALLING . . . I AM CALLED

77

> For surely I know the plans I have for you, says the Lord, plans for your welfare and not for harm, to give you a future with hope.
>
> —JEREMIAH 29:11

One of the biggest blocks to hearing God's call is our pride. We may feel God's nudges in our hearts and minds, but we think we know better. *I don't need God,* we tell ourselves. *I'm gonna do what I want, when I want, because I want to.*

Our selfishness grows the more we feed it. As it spreads, it separates us from God and from being who we really are. It separates us from others too. Because no one likes hanging out with someone who only thinks about, talks about, or cares about themselves. Am I right?

The truth is, prideful people make gods of themselves. They worship their image and want others to do the same. It might seem shiny and maybe even attractive at first—but in reality, it's completely fake and hollow. And when we let our sense of worth completely depend on the admiration and praise of others, no matter how much attention we get, it's never enough. It can't be. That's because our greatest want and deepest need is for God. Ignoring it, denying it, or trying to fill it by being so full of ourselves doesn't change the fact we are made for God. And God alone can fill us.

God wants to help us realize how much he loves us and how much we need him. He wants us to realize all we can be with his help. That's why he will never stop calling us to him. No matter how we may be sleepwalking through life, God will never stop nudging our hearts awake because he has so much more to give us. If we focus on ourselves, we will only ever see what we lack.

But if we focus on God, he will fill us to overflowing.

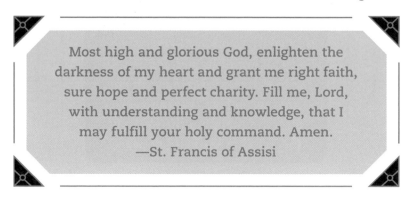

Most high and glorious God, enlighten the darkness of my heart and grant me right faith, sure hope and perfect charity. Fill me, Lord, with understanding and knowledge, that I may fulfill your holy command. Amen.
—St. Francis of Assisi

Digging Deeper

1. In what way might pride be holding you back from all that God wants to give you?
2. How might your pride be affecting your relationships with others?

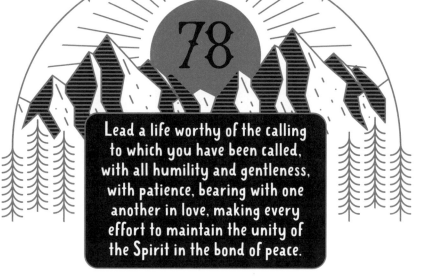

GOD IS CALLING ... I AM CALLED

78

Lead a life worthy of the calling to which you have been called, with all humility and gentleness, with patience, bearing with one another in love, making every effort to maintain the unity of the Spirit in the bond of peace.

—EPHESIANS 4:1–3

We've explored how God created us for a purpose. He gave us these specific gifts, interests, and personality for this exact life. It all helps us become the person he had in mind when he created us—that best version of ourselves.

Sounds like some kind of saint.

Exactly. That ideal version God had in mind for each of us is the saint we can become with God's help. Because we are all called to be saints, and it is possible for each of us. Even the most holy of saints were ordinary people like us. They faced challenges, they doubted, and they sinned. But in the midst of their ups and downs, they persevered in pleasing God, not others. In their unique circumstances, they learned to rely on God's mercy, guidance, and grace. Step by step, the closer each became with God, the more they grew in holiness.

Over ten thousand saints are recognized by the Church. These men and women come from different generations, countries, and classes. They dedicated themselves to God at different ages and had different gifts. Some were teachers, writers, or musicians, others were scientists, students, or soldiers. Even their ministries are very different. But they all share something—a deep love for the Lord. Through that relationship, God helped each understand and use their unique gifts so they could make a difference for others and change the world for the better. Just by being themselves. Just by fully becoming the person God made them to be.

Every saint is different, and yet all are perfect examples of holiness and of what is possible when we walk with God.

> God, forgive me for the ways I let the opinions of others shape how I act, what I think, and how I feel. Help me to live to please you alone, because that is the way to holiness and true joy. Amen.

Digging Deeper

What saint are you curious about? Maybe you heard a bit about their life and witness or felt moved by one of their quotes. Follow that spiritual nudge. Learn about their life and faith. Pray with them and ask them to pray for your special intentions.

The saints were so completely dead to themselves that they cared very little whether others agreed with them or not.
—St. John Vianney

GOD IS CALLING . . . I AM CALLED

R&R: Rest and Remember

Look back over what you read and wrote this week. What's your main takeaway?

_____

_____

_____

_____

_____

_____

_____

_____

_____

_____

WHY I CAN DO IT

GOD IS JESUS . . . I AM SAVED

Lord Jesus, let me know myself and know you, and desire nothing save only you . . . Let me do everything for the sake of you. Let me humble myself and exalt you . . . Let me be among those who are chosen by you . . . Look upon me, that I may love you. Call me that I may see you, and for ever enjoy you. Amen.

—EXCERPT OF A PRAYER BY ST. AUGUSTINE

GOD IS JESUS ... I AM SAVED

79

He said to them,
"Come and see."

—JOHN 1:39

Jesus's first words in the Gospel of John appear when he first meets his future disciples and asks them, "What are you looking for?" It's the story of how they met. But it's our story too. Because today, Jesus asks each one of us: *What are you looking for?*

Sure, we always want things: The latest phone. A new bike. Those shoes everyone has. The list keeps changing, right? But this is a bigger question. It's like Jesus is looking deep into our eyes and asking: *What is missing in your life? What do you really want? What does your heart need?*

It's the kind of question we have to sit with before we come to an honest answer, because we might not even know. But it's definitely worth thinking about. Are we lonely or hurting? Are we bored, lost, or confused in some way? We might feel ashamed of something in our past or be anxious about the future. Maybe we feel really overwhelmed and tired. But whatever we need, Jesus wants to help. How?

"Come and see," Jesus says.

Can you hear the excitement in his voice? He knows the wonderful things that lay ahead. When Jesus calls those first disciples, he is also giving an open invitation to go with him and see for ourselves. It's like he is saying: *Come with me. Come and learn from me. Come and see what I have for you.*

Jesus wants to help us discover what our heart really needs. The more we walk and talk with him, the more we learn about those deepest needs—and how Jesus meets them.

Jesus, I want to learn from you. I want to receive all that you want to give me. I want to be all that you know I can be. Thank you for your invitation to come and see. Amen.

Digging Deeper

St. Ignatius encourages us to picture ourselves actually *in* the gospel story. You are there when Jesus feeds the five thousand, when he heals the lame, or in this case when he first meets his disciples. What does it sound like, feel like, look like to be there? Picture him coming up to you and inviting you to come and see. What does he do? How does he look at you? How will you respond?

After you've spent time in imaginative prayer, write about that experience.

Dear young people . . . in saying "yes" to Christ, you say "yes" to all your noblest ideals. I pray that he will reign in your hearts . . . Have no fear of entrusting yourselves to him! He will guide you, he will grant you the strength to follow him every day and in every situation.

—St. Pope John Paul II

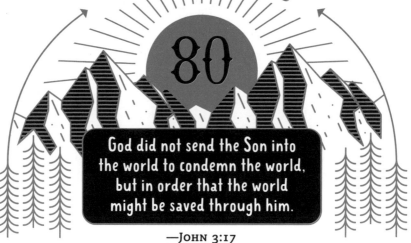

80

> God did not send the Son into the world to condemn the world, but in order that the world might be saved through him.
>
> —JOHN 3:17

Jesus sure knew how to stir things up. Instead of trying to fit in with popular or powerful individuals, Jesus hung out with Zacchaeus—the guy nobody liked. Jesus stood up for a woman the crowd wanted to stone. He reached out to the lepers even though they were shunned. People must have wondered, *What's he thinking?*

But Jesus didn't follow the crowd. He didn't give in to peer pressure or do things to just fit in and be liked. He wasn't thinking about himself at all, actually. Jesus's mind was always on the person before him. That lonely guy. That scared girl. That person everyone ignored. While others judged them for their flaws—Jesus simply loved them for their hearts.

Love. It's why Jesus saved Zacchaeus, the woman, and the lepers. It's why he saved us too.

Jesus loved us enough to come to earth and become human so we might know God better. Through he was all-powerful, Jesus loved us enough to humbly surrender his life for us. He paid for our sins at great cost and great pain. Jesus endured all of that to give us life with God forever.

Jesus showed us what love is. He taught us what love does. And he promised to be with us always, helping us love God and each other.

Jesus, I admit sometimes I go along with the crowd even though my heart tells me it's wrong. Give me your courage so I become more like you. Help me to hang out with, stand up for, and reach out to someone who needs it today. Amen.

Digging Deeper

1. Who are you in those gospel stories? The popular and powerful? The judged and excluded?
2. What do you think Jesus would say to you?
3. How can you be more like Jesus in the way you treat others?

What really matters in life is that we are loved by Christ and that we love him in return. In comparison to the love of Jesus, everything else is secondary. And, without the love of Jesus, everything is useless.

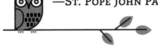

—St. Pope John Paul II

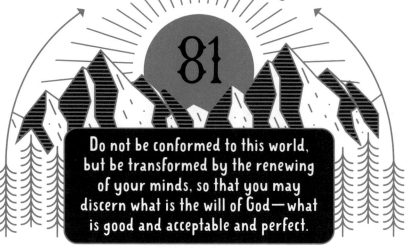

GOD IS JESUS . . . I AM SAVED

81

> Do not be conformed to this world, but be transformed by the renewing of your minds, so that you may discern what is the will of God—what is good and acceptable and perfect.

—ROMANS 12:2

A mind is a powerful tool. It's where ideas begin and plans are formed. Our minds determine our attitude and perceptions. *Is the glass half empty or half full? Is this challenge or an opportunity? Was that a total failure or a life lesson?* Our minds even determine how we see ourselves.

It's funny that, even though our brains are so powerful, we don't think about *how we think* all that much. But the mind affects so much of our lives. It shapes our understanding (or misunderstanding), it swings our moods, it often controls our choices. Our minds can determine the quality of both our lives and our characters. But despite all of this, the mind is still only a *tool*. That means we decide how to use it.

So why not use it for good?

God gave us our minds, but he also gave us our will. Our will helps us control our thoughts so our thoughts don't control us. We don't have to be at the mercy of worry, fear, or other negative imaginings. We can choose to see things positively.

We can pray and know that God will help. He will renew our minds, and because of it we'll be changed for the better.

When we fill our minds with God's truth, Jesus's example and teachings, and the Holy Spirit's grace, we'll start to notice a real shift in our lives. As Christ's life grows in us, we'll see the blessings and feel more blessed and feel more joyful and peaceful. We'll have more courage and confidence. Not only will our struggles seem less overwhelming, we'll start to see their blessings in disguise.

Jesus Christ, in his infinite love, has become what we are in order that he may make us entirely what he is.

—St. Irenaeus

Jesus, fill my heart and inspire my mind to be more and more like yours. Amen.

Digging Deeper

1. Do your thoughts build up or tear down?
2. Your mind is powerful. In what ways could you be using this tool more for good?

82

As the Father has loved me, so I have loved you; abide in my love. If you keep my commandments, you will abide in my love.

—JOHN 15:9–11

Whenever we get an assigned school project, it really helps if the teacher shows us examples. Not only does it make her expectations clear, those examples inspire us. Just seeing that good work helps us to come up with creative ways we can share our ideas.

God does the same for us in this project called life. God the Father sent his Son, Jesus, to be our inspiration. It's like God is saying: *Look at what Jesus does, forgive like he forgives, serve like he serves, love like he loves.* Jesus is our A+ example.

Knowing Jesus better—through the Gospels, prayer, and the sacraments—helps us to follow his example. We realize he wasn't interested in popularity or power. He didn't care about what he wore or owned. All that really mattered to him was the *people.* Jesus never stopped reaching out to help someone in need. To give hope. To feed the hungry. To include the lonely. Time after time, in the person before him, Jesus saw a need and met it.

That's what love is. That's what love does.

Before he returned to the Father, Jesus entrusted his

mission of love to us. That means we are called to be there for the person before us. It means seeing their needs and coming up with creative ways to meet them. It means asking: *How can I help? What can I do to include them? In what ways can I be there for them?*

Thankfully, we have Jesus and the Holy Spirit as our "life project" partners. When we remember that, and invite them into our brainstorming, we'll be amazed and what we can imagine and achieve together.

> Jesus, thank you for being my example and my guide. Thank you for sending the Holy Spirit to help me live and love as you taught. Help me to be more like you in how I treat others. Amen.

1. What qualities of Jesus inspire you?
2. In what specific ways can you love more like Jesus?

With Christ's life in you, you can begin to love God and the people in your life in a way that you could not do on your own, for it is Christ loving them through you.

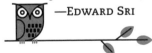 —EDWARD SRI

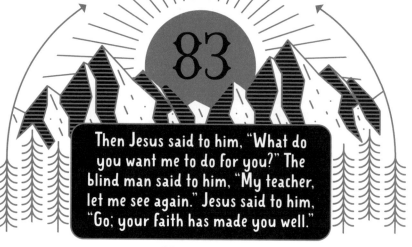

GOD IS JESUS...I AM SAVED

83

Then Jesus said to him, "What do you want me to do for you?" The blind man said to him, "My teacher, let me see again." Jesus said to him, "Go; your faith has made you well."

—MARK 10:51–52

Why does Jesus ask what this blind man, Bartimaeus, wants? Bartimaeus spent his life begging on the side of the road because of his blindness and poverty. No doubt, Jesus already knew the guy wanted to see, but he also knew how important it was for Bartimaeus to *ask* for his help. Doing so meant Bartimaeus was coming to Jesus with his needs, and knew Jesus well enough to ask full of hope.

That's what prayer is. When we pray, we answer Jesus's call to come to him. And every time, Jesus asks us: *What do you want me to do for you?*

Jesus sees our hearts and needs as clearly as he noticed Bartimaeus's blindness, which means we aren't telling him anything he doesn't already know. But by asking, Jesus is helping us discover what we really want. We might feel angry at a friend, but as we bring it to Jesus and talk about it, he helps us realize our heart is actually more hurt than angry. And so we ask Jesus to help heal the friendship. Or maybe we feel really anxious about a situation we want to control. Just telling Jesus about it can help us realize that we can let go. Time with Jesus always opens our eyes and our hearts. Like Bartimaeus, we can always call on Jesus, we can come to him full of hope and ask, "My teacher, let me see again."

> Shine through me and be so in me that every soul I come in contact with may feel your presence in my soul. Let them look up and see no longer me but only Jesus.
> —St. Teresa of Calcutta's adaptation of Blessed John Henry Newman's prayer

Digging Deeper

Prayerfully reread St. Pope John Paul's quote or the prayer. What part is most meaningful to you right now? Why?

It is Jesus in fact that you seek when you dream of happiness; he is waiting for you when nothing else you find satisfies you; he is the beauty to which you are so attracted; it is he who provokes you with that thirst for fullness that will not let you settle for compromise; it is he who urges you to shed the masks of a false life . . . It is Jesus who stirs in you the desire to do something great with your lives.
—ST. POPE JOHN PAUL II

GOD IS JESUS... I AM SAVED

84

A sower went out to sow his seed;
and as he sowed, some fell on the
path and was trampled on, and
the birds of the air ate it up. Some
fell on the rock; and as it grew up,
it withered for lack of moisture.
Some fell among thorns and the
thorns grew with it and choked it.
Some fell into good soil, and when it
grew, it produced a hundredfold.

—LUKE 8:5–8

We read the Bible sometimes. We go to mass now and then. We pray when we remember to pray (mostly when we want something). But for some reason, our faith doesn't feel all that fruitful. Ever wonder why?

Jesus explains that God's Word is like seed, generously scattered all over. The seed is always the same, but the results vary. Some seed shrivels up on rocky ground, some can't grow because of all the weeds and thorns, and other seed takes root and spreads into a bumper crop. It all depends on the soil.

It's the same with our faith. If we want God's Word to be fruitful in our lives, we need to be good soil. That means noticing what God is already doing for us and remembering what he has done, then letting it take root in our hearts. It means making God the center of our lives and weeding out anything that tries to take his place. We make the Word a priority. We read it regularly and think about it deeply. We pray daily. And we receive the sacraments of Reconciliation and the Eucharist often.

That's how our relationship with Jesus deepens and grows. It's how we become more and more like him. And *knowing about* Jesus isn't the same as *knowing* Jesus. Our personal relationship saves us, yes, but it also changes us. Jesus doesn't just give us God's Word, he *is* the Word.[1] So the more we work at being good soil, the more Jesus grows in us and spreads through us.

> Jesus, I know you in my head, but I want to feel you in my heart. Help me to know you better and better. Show me how to become good soil that grows a deep-rooted and fruitful faith. Amen.

Digging Deeper

1. Read Jesus's parable about the sower in Luke 8:5–8 and his explanation of what it means in Luke 8:11–15. What kind of soil are you?
2. What can you do to help you become good soil for God's Word?

The most beautiful and stirring adventure that can happen to you is the personal meeting with Jesus, who is the only one who gives real meaning to our lives.

—St. Pope John Paul II

---

1. John 1:1

GOD IS JESUS ... I AM SAVED

R&R: Rest and Remember

Look back over what you read and wrote this week. What's your main takeaway?

_____

_____

_____

_____

_____

_____

_____

_____

_____

_____

WHY I CAN DO IT

GOD IS SPIRIT . . . I AM SENT

Send me, Lord, wherever you please, for when I am sent by you, then I am quite sure that you will help me—in whatever situation I find myself—to fulfil what you ask.
Amen.

—St. Francis de Sales

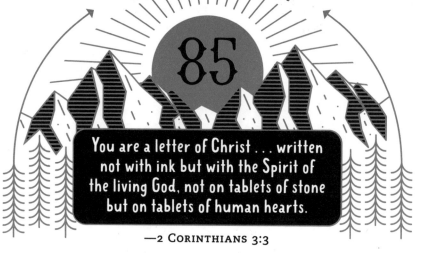

GOD IS SPIRIT . . . I AM SENT

85

You are a letter of Christ . . . written not with ink but with the Spirit of the living God, not on tablets of stone but on tablets of human hearts.

—2 CORINTHIANS 3:3

God speaks to the world through the Bible, but he also speaks through us. We are God's letters to the world. By our words and actions, we let others know how much they mean to us and to God. So what kind of message are we sending?

We wouldn't write someone a letter that said, *You're so annoying. No one likes you.* Or send them a brightly colored card that read, *Ugh. Don't even talk to me. I'm way better than you.* Or what a postcard that said, *Hey! Having a wonderful time without you, loser.* That's just mean.

But for some reason, we send those messages out every day. We don't write it—or even say it—but people read it loud and clear in the way we look at them and the way we treat them. Even if we just ignored them altogether, that exclusion and dismissiveness would say more than any five-page letter ever could: *You're not important. You don't matter. No one cares about you.*

God wants his Spirit to work in us so we become his love letter to others, one of love, kindness, and inclusion. He wants what others read in us to leave them feeling like they matter and belong. Because they do.

It can be as simple as a smile, a hello, or looking them in the eyes and really listening when they speak. Every interaction sends a message.

Spread love everywhere you go. Let no one ever come to you without leaving happier.

—St. Teresa of Calcutta

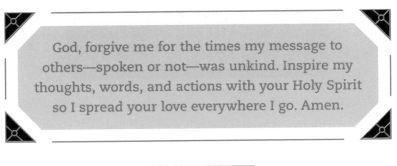

It's up to us to ensure that the message we are sending is what God really wants to say.

> God, forgive me for the times my message to others—spoken or not—was unkind. Inspire my thoughts, words, and actions with your Holy Spirit so I spread your love everywhere I go. Amen.

Digging Deeper

1. When people hang out with you or chat with you, do they leave happier?
2. What's one small thing you can do to make people feel welcomed, accepted, cherished, or happier?

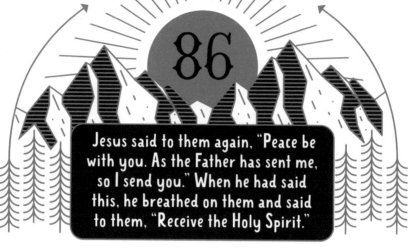

GOD IS SPIRIT . . . I AM SENT

86

> Jesus said to them again, "Peace be with you. As the Father has sent me, so I send you." When he had said this, he breathed on them and said to them, "Receive the Holy Spirit."

—JOHN 20:21–22

Jesus came to save us, teach us, and change us little by little into the best version of ourselves. But he also came to *send* us. Because God's love is not just for us—it's for the world. That's our mission, and it's not a secret mission or even a mission impossible.

Jesus started the work. Before he returned to heaven, he passed this mission to his twelve apostles, to the Church. They gave it the men, women, and children who followed Jesus, and it has been passed from generation to generation ever since.

A big part of that mission is to *witness*. Jesus wants us to share what we know about him and about God's love and mercy. Of course, we can't share what we don't have, so another big part of our mission is to *keep growing in faith* ourselves. To pray. To read Scripture. To receive the sacraments, and to walk with Jesus every day of our lives.

Witnessing just means sharing our story with a friend in need. Being open and honest about a time when God helped us inspires people who may be lost or struggling to turn to

God for help too. What's more, the Holy Spirit inspires us as we share. He gives us the opportunities, the courage, and even the words when we need them. The more we stay open to the Spirit, the more he will work in and through us. Think of it like a flame passed from one candle to the next, as person by person the world becomes a brighter place.

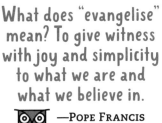

What does "evangelise" mean? To give witness with joy and simplicity to what we are and what we believe in.

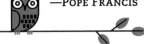

—POPE FRANCIS

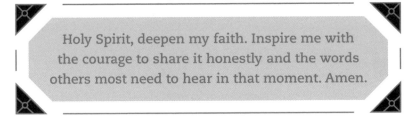

Holy Spirit, deepen my faith. Inspire me with the courage to share it honestly and the words others most need to hear in that moment. Amen.

Digging Deeper

Write about a time when God helped you. Getting it down will help you to feel more comfortable in getting it out and sharing it with someone in need.

GOD IS SPIRIT ... I AM SENT

87

As you have sent me into the world, so I have sent them into the world.

—JOHN 17:18

Witnessing and sharing our stories is part of the mission Jesus gives us. Another big part of it is justice. Jesus shows us that love isn't only expressed in words—it's shown in action. That's what justice is. It's why Jesus defends the victim from the angry crowd. It's why he helps the sick. It's why he goes out of his way to include the lost and ignored. Because he loves.

Even in his parables, Jesus shows love is why the Good Samaritan helps the injured man, why the father welcomes home his runaway son with open arms, and why the Good Shepherd doesn't stop searching for his lost lamb. These weren't campfire stories Jesus told to entertain the crowd. They are simple yet powerful examples that teach us about God's profound love in a way we understand.

In Matthew 25, Jesus gives his most powerful teaching on justice. He says, "I was hungry and you gave me food, I was thirsty and you gave me something to drink, I was a stranger and you welcomed me, I was naked and you gave me clothing, I was sick and you took care of me, I was in prison and you visited me."[1] That's because justice means doing what we

---

1.   Matthew 25:35–36

can to help others in need. It's feeding the hungry, welcoming the stranger, and caring for the sick. It's sharing our resources and time. But justice also means standing up for the defenseless, speaking up for the voiceless, and making sure every person is treated with dignity and respect. We do it at home and at school. We do it in our community, city, and country. We do it worldwide.

And every time we do, we do it for Jesus.

Do you want to do something beautiful for God? There is a person who needs you. This is your chance.

—St. Teresa of Calcutta

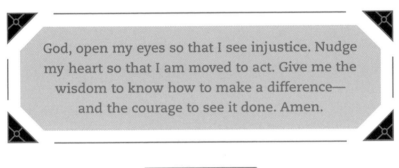

God, open my eyes so that I see injustice. Nudge my heart so that I am moved to act. Give me the wisdom to know how to make a difference— and the courage to see it done. Amen.

Digging Deeper

1. Is someone you know struggling or in need? Is there an injustice that currently weighs upon your heart?
2. What is one thing you can do to make a difference? Make a plan to do it. Take that first step.

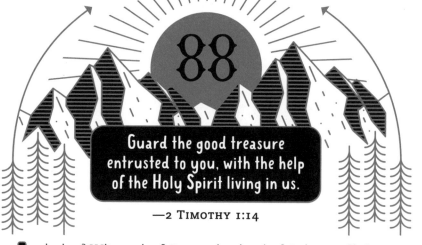

GOD IS SPIRIT ... I AM SENT

88

Guard the good treasure entrusted to you, with the help of the Holy Spirit living in us.

—2 TIMOTHY 1:14

Amission? Witnessing? Promoting justice? Being God's letter to the world? Being a Christian does come with a lot of responsibilities—but, honestly, the benefits are totally worth it. Besides, it's not like we have to do any of it alone. We have one another. We have the Church. And most importantly, we have the Holy Spirit on our side.

Our *inside*.

It's mind-blowing when you think about it, really. The Spirit of God, the all-powerful Creator of the universe, lives *inside* us. He works in us. He empowers and inspires us. He transforms us to be more and more like Jesus. He helps us grow in holiness, grow closer to God and one another, and to bear good fruit—things like peace, patience, kindness, goodness, faithfulness, gentleness, self-control, love, and overflowing joy.

That's *if* we are open to him. God may be all-powerful, but he won't barge in. He doesn't take over control of our lives and minds. He won't manipulate us or force us to do his will. Why? Because that isn't loving—and God is love. Love guides, encourages, invites—and then waits for our response. God calls us closer because he loves us. He sends us to be that love to others. And through his Spirit, he helps us to love him, love others, and love ourselves.

The Holy Spirit, the love of God, acts in our spirit . . . He is the very love of God, who does not abandon us.

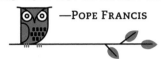

—POPE FRANCIS

It's all our choice, and, yes, our responsibility. But the more we think about that incredible opportunity to have a personal relationship with God—the more we'll see it's a wonderful treasure.

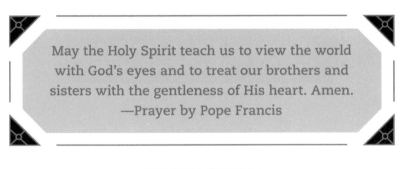

May the Holy Spirit teach us to view the world with God's eyes and to treat our brothers and sisters with the gentleness of His heart. Amen.
—Prayer by Pope Francis

Digging Deeper

Thank God for all the ways he guides, supports, and inspires you as you grow in faith:

1. Thank him for your friends and family
2. Thank him for your Church and school communities
3. Above all, thank him for his Holy Spirit at work in, with, and through you

GOD IS SPIRIT ... I AM SENT

89

You are the light of the world. A city built on a hill cannot be hid ... Let your light shine before others, so that they may see your good works and give glory to your Father in heaven.

—MATTHEW 5:14–16

God sends us into the world to shine. To bring light and hope. To stir wonder and joy just by being who we are. But are we shining our brightest? What keeps us from our fullest potential?

Sometimes the brightness of others makes us doubt that we have anything worth sharing. *I'll never be as [smart/funny/ creative/friendly/good] as her. So why bother trying?* But God doesn't want us to be like anyone else. The world needs the light only we can bring, and we shine brightest when we shine in our own way.

Sometimes we choose not to shine for fear of being criticized or judged by others. Afraid of being judged, mocked, or rejected, we dim our unique brilliance or think we're a dud bulb. But imagine how much brighter the world would be if we all stopped worrying much about what others think and do, and started living by what God actually says: "You are the light of the world . . . Let your light shine."

Just because we haven't fully sparkled yet doesn't mean we can't. If we ask the Holy Spirit, he will help us see how and where we can best shine.

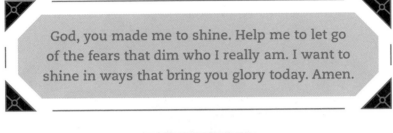

God, you made me to shine. Help me to let go of the fears that dim who I really am. I want to shine in ways that bring you glory today. Amen.

Digging Deeper

1. What is your unique brilliance?
2. What beliefs have made you dim your light?
3. How will you get past that belief and shine bright?

> Dear young people, let yourselves be taken over by the light of Christ and spread that light wherever you are.
>
> —St. Pope John Paul II

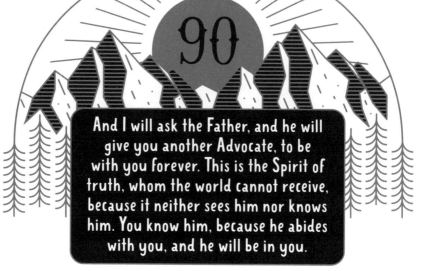

GOD IS SPIRIT... I AM SENT

90

And I will ask the Father, and he will give you another Advocate, to be with you forever. This is the Spirit of truth, whom the world cannot receive, because it neither sees him nor knows him. You know him, because he abides with you, and he will be in you.

—JOHN 14:16–17

The Holy Spirit is a generous giver—he's also a generous gift. Before he returned to heaven, Jesus asked God to send us the Holy Spirit. Because of that gift, the Spirit actually lives in us. Day after day, he gives us the abilities, guidance, and grace we need to grow in holiness, the wisdom we need to know God's will, and the courage, strength, and commitment to do it. He gives us the right words to encourage others[1] and helps us in prayer.[2]

When he came at Pentecost, the Holy Spirit helped the apostles establish a Church that has lasted two thousand years. The Spirit inspired Scripture and continues to inspire us as we read it. It's because of the Holy Spirit's work billions of Christians exist worldwide today. He is relentless, ever-present, and eager to work with us, in us, and through us.

1. Luke 12:12
2. Romans 8:26

Our baptism made us Christian and—with the Holy Spirit's help—we become Christlike, little by little, for the rest of our lives. Because being Christian isn't a box checked. It's an invitation to a lifelong adventure.

Thanks to God's master plan—with Christ as our foundation[3] and the Holy Spirit as our help[4]—we can live an amazing life as we work together to build one just and peaceful world.

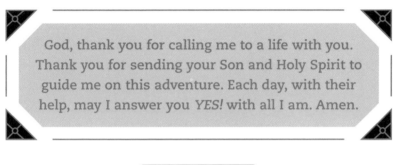

God, thank you for calling me to a life with you. Thank you for sending your Son and Holy Spirit to guide me on this adventure. Each day, with their help, may I answer you *YES!* with all I am. Amen.

Digging Deeper

1. How does it change your outlook to see faith as a lifelong journey with the One who loves us most?
2. How does it feel to be entrusted with the wonderful task of building a civilization of love?
3. In what big and small ways are you already doing your part? What more can you do?

Allow me, dear young people, to consign this hope of mine to you: you must be those "builders"! . . . The future is in your hearts and in your hands. God is entrusting to you the task, at once difficult and uplifting, of working with him in the building of the civilization of love.

—St. Pope John Paul II

---

3. Ephesians 2:19–22
4. John 14:16–17

GOD IS SPIRIT . . . I AM SENT

R&R: Rest and Remember

Look back over what you read and wrote this week. What's your main takeaway?

_____

_____

_____

_____

_____

_____

_____

_____

_____

_____

_____

EXAMINATION OF CONSCIENCE

Do a regular examination of conscience using the Ten Commandments. You can do all ten or choose one thing a day to focus on in your journal.

1. Have I let anything or anyone else be more important to me than God?
2. Do I ever use God's name as a curse word?
3. Do I treat Sunday as God's day of rest? Do I go to mass?
4. Do I respect my parents? Do I criticize them to my friends? Do I do my part at home?
5. Have I hurt others by my words or actions? Have I hurt myself? Are there things I do that keep me or others from growing in healthiness and holiness?
6. Do I respect my body? Do I respect the bodies of others by my words, actions, and thoughts?
7. Have I stolen or cheated? Am I fair in how I spend my time, talents, and money?
8. Do I gossip? When I hear a rumor, do I stop it?
9. Do I promote things (movies, books, shows, music, videos) that degrade others?
10. Am I jealous? Do I envy others for their good things?

WHERE TO LOOK WHEN I FEEL ...

WHERE TO LOOK WHEN I WONDER ...

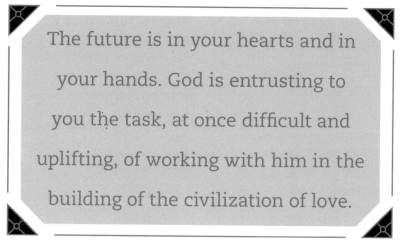

The future is in your hearts and in your hands. God is entrusting to you the task, at once difficult and uplifting, of working with him in the building of the civilization of love.

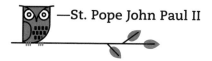 —St. Pope John Paul II